GREAT AMERICAN STORIES 2

Second Edition

beginning-intermediate to upper-intermediate levels

C. G. Draper

D0145276

Prentice Hall Regents
Englewood Cliffs, New Jersey 07632

Library of Congress Cataloging-in-Publication Data

Draper, C. G.
   Great American stories : an ESL/EFL reader: beginning
-intermediate to upper-intermediate levels / C. G. Draper.
      p.   cm.
   ISBN 0-13-097528-1
   1. English language–Textbooks for foreign speakers. 2. Short
stories, American–Adaptations. 3. Readers–United States.
   I. Title.
   PE1128.D675   1994
   428.6'4–dc20

Editorial Director: Arley Gray
Acquisitions Editor: Nancy Leonhardt
Director of Production and Manufacturing: David Riccardi
Electronic Production Coordinator: Molly Pike Riccardi
Creative Director: Paula Maylahn

Editorial Production/Design Manager: Dominick Mosco
Electronic/Production Supervision, Page Composition and
   Interior Design: Noël Vreeland Carter
Cover Design Coordinator: Merle Krumper
Cover Design: Jayne Conte
Production Coordinator: Ray Keating

Cover and Interior Illustrations: Len Shalansky

"The Lost Phoebe" pp. 115–128 printed by permission of
The Dreiser Trust, Harold J. Dies, Trustee

Prentice-Hall International (UK) Limited, *London*
Prentice-Hall of Australia Pty. Limited, *Sydney*
Prentice-Hall of Canada Inc. *Toronto*
Prentice-Hall Hispanoamericana, S.A., *Mexico*
Prentice-Hall of India Private Limited, *New Delhi*
Prentice-Hall of Japan, Inc. *Tokyo*
Simon & Schuster Asia Pte. Ltd., *Singapore*
Editora Prentice-Hall do Brasil, Ltda., *Rio de Janeiro*

CONTENTS

TO THE READER

This book starts at the intermediate level and ends at the upper-intermediate level. The seven stories in the book steadily increase in difficulty. The vocabulary list for the first story contains 1000 words; for the second and third stories, 1250 words; and for the final four stories, 1500 words. The length of the sentences increases, and new grammar is introduced with each story.

By working on this book, you will improve your
- reading
- speaking and discussion
- vocabulary
- knowledge of word forms
- writing

Each story in the book is divided into two to four parts or sections. Following the story, there is an exercise (Exercise A: Understanding the Plot of the Story) that is based on the whole story. This exercise is followed by other exercises for each separate section of the story, based on the material in that section. You should try to read the whole story before beginning any of the exercises. If you find Exercise A difficult, re-read the story by sections, and do the exercises for one section before reading the next section. After finishing all the other exercises, try again to do Exercise A.

The exercises will help you develop your language skills in general and your reading skills in particular. Most of the exercises are on reading comprehension, vocabulary, word forms, discussion, and writing. Several of them will introduce you to some of the more difficult elements of written English: irony of situation, irony of expression, inference, hidden meaning, and figurative language.

The stories in this book were written many years ago by seven of America's most famous writers. You will read about the writers' lives before you read their stories. Special exercises will introduce you to the world of each story before you read it. Good luck and good reading!

TO THE TEACHER

GREAT AMERICAN STORIES 2 consists of seven careful adaptations of famous stories by classic American writers and exercises for each story in reading skills, vocabulary, word forms, language activities, writing and discussion. Prereading exercises introduce the student to the world in which the story takes place and explore the biographical information provided about each writer on the title page of each story.

The book is both graded and progressive—that is, the vocabulary, grammar, and internal structure of the stories increase in difficulty from the first story (which is at the beginning-intermediate level of proficiency) to the last (which is at the upper-intermediate level). Structural, lexical, and sentence-length controls have been used throughout the book. The head-word list for the first story contains 1000 words; for the second and third stories, 1250 words; and for the final stories, 1500 words. Maximum sentence length increases from 15 words in the first story to 20 in the last, and new grammatical structures are added story by story. Words from outside the head-word lists are introduced in a context that helps make their meaning clear; they are used again within the next 100 words of text and then repeated at least two more times before the end of the story.

The book as a whole is designed to be incorporated into a 12- to 14-week course in ESL or EFL as part of the reading program. The material can be used either in or out of class—as a core reading text, ancillary text, or simply for pleasure reading. Its in-class use can take a number of different forms: teacher-student, student-student (pairs or small groups), student-tutor, or student alone.

Like the stories, the exercises in the book increase in difficulty, gradually introducing the student to the more demanding elements of English prose that characterize unabridged or advanced texts: irony of situation and expression, implication and inference, hidden meaning, figurative language, and so on. Further, the exercises are so designed that the student must constantly return to the text to check comprehension or vocabulary. An objective of the book is to involve the reader deeply in the text of each story and the world of its writer, and, toward that end, to present exercises that are difficult if not impossible to complete without a thorough understanding of the text.

Each story is divided into two to four parts, or sections. The first exercise following each story, "Exercise A: Understanding the Plot of the Story," encompasses the entire story. Thereafter, the exercises in vocabulary, word forms, language activities, and writing are based on the sub-sections of the story. The concluding Discussion exercise returns to the story as a whole and asks the student to comment on its major themes. It is best, therefore, to have the student read through the entire story once, share first impressions, and attempt Exercise A; and then re-read each section carefully and work on the exercises based on the material in that section. The first long reading "stretches" the student; the re-reading and exercises consolidate gains and help the student achieve complete familiarity with the materials. If the student has trouble with Exercise A the first time around, he or she should be asked to repeat it after the other exercises, but before the Discussion exercise.

Both an Answer Key, and a cassette of the stories read aloud, are available from the publisher.

C.G.D.

THE ROMANCE OF A BUSY BROKER

Before You Read the Story ...

1. *A Life*

Read the paragraph about O. Henry on page 3. What do you notice about his work experience? What could you expect the characters in his stories to be like?

2. *The Picture*

The picture on page 5 shows us the office of a *stockbroker*, that is, a person who buys and sells pieces of businesses (called *stocks*, or *shares*) for customers. In the picture, the stockbroker is standing behind his desk. On the desk is a telephone and a *ticker tape machine*. The ticker tape machine prints the prices of stocks on a paper *tape*.

Do you think this picture shows an office of 1900, 1950, or 1990? Why do you think so? What machines would you expect to see in a stockbroker's office today?

3. *Thinking About It ...*

What do you like, or dislike, about the world of business? Why? Which of the following words or phrases best describe the business world to you: peaceful, exciting, full of pressure, beautiful, interesting, dangerous, busy, slow, loving, restful, fast. Are you a businessman or a businesswoman? Would you like to become one?

4. *Scanning for Specific Information*

Read the questions below. The answer to each question can be found in the paragraph about O. Henry on page 3. As you read the paragraph, look for the piece of information that will answer the question. You do not need to understand everything in the paragraph. But you must read carefully enough to find the answer to each question. This kind of reading to find specific information is called *scanning*. Try to answer each question in 30 seconds or less.

a. In what state was O. Henry born?
b. In what year did he leave school?
c. How many jobs did he have before he began writing?
d. Where was O. Henry when he published his first book?
e. What kind of book was it?
f. What kind of stories is O. Henry most famous for?
g. What kind of people usually appear in his stories?
h. Who was William Sydney Porter?

THE ROMANCE OF A BUSY BROKER

adapted from the story by

O. HENRY

O. Henry was born in Greensboro, North Carolina, in 1862. His real name was William Sydney Porter. He left school at fifteen and worked at different times in a drug store, a business office, an architect's office, and finally a bank. When he was caught taking money from his own bank, he was arrested and put in prison for three years. He had begun writing, and while he was in prison he published a book of adventure stories called Cabbages and Kings. He moved to New York in 1902, and it was there that he became famous for his short stories with surprise endings. He wrote hundreds of stories about the ordinary people of New York City. His most famous books include The Four Million and The Voice of the City. O. Henry died in 1910.

I

Pitcher had worked for many years in the office of Harvey Maxwell, the stockbroker. Pitcher was a quiet man. He didn't usually let his face show his feelings. But this morning he looked surprised—and very interested. Harvey Maxwell had arrived energetically as usual at 9:30. But this morning, the young lady who was his secretary had arrived with him. Pitcher watched them with interest. Harvey Maxwell didn't pay attention to Pitcher. He said only a quick "Good morning," and ran to his desk. He dug energetically into the mountain of letters and telegrams that waited for him.

2 The young lady had been the stockbroker's secretary for a year. She was beautiful, and she dressed simply. Unlike some secretaries, she never wore cheap glass jewelry. Her dress was grey and plain, but it fitted her body nicely. With it she wore a small black hat with a green-gold flower at the side. This morning her face shone with happiness. Her eyes were bright, her face a soft pink.

3 Pitcher, still interested, noticed that she acted differently this morning. Usually she walked straight inside to her own desk. But this morning she stayed in the outside office. She walked over near Maxwell's desk. Maxwell didn't seem to be a man anymore. He had changed into a busy New York stockbroker. He'd become a machine of many moving parts.

4 "Well—what is it? Is anything wrong?" Maxwell asked his secretary. He wasn't looking at her. His eyes were on his mail. Letters and telegrams lay on his desk like snow.

5 "It's nothing," she said softly. She moved away with a little smile. "Mr. Pitcher," she said, coming over to him,

"did Mr. Maxwell ask you to hire another secretary yesterday?"

6 "Yes, he did," answered Pitcher. "He told me to get another one. I asked the secretarial school to send over a few this morning. But it's 9:45, and no one has come yet."

7 "I will do the work as usual, then," said the young lady, "until someone comes to fill the place." And she went to her desk at once. She hung up the black hat with the green-gold flower in its usual place.

8 Harvey Maxwell was always a busy stockbroker, but today he was even busier than usual. The ticker tape machine began to throw out tape. The desk telephone began to ring. Men crowded into the office, buying and selling, crying and yelling. Boys ran in and out with telegrams. Even Pitcher's face looked more alive. Maxwell pushed his chair against the wall. He ran energetically from ticker tape to telephone, jumping like a dancer.

9 In the middle of all this action and yelling, the stockbroker realized that someone new had arrived. He first saw a high mountain of golden hair under a large round hat. Then he noticed some large glass jewelry. Underneath all this was a young lady. Pitcher saw that Maxwell didn't know who she was. He came forward to explain. "Here is the lady from the secretarial school," Pitcher said to Maxwell. "She came for the job."

10 Maxwell turned around with his hands full of papers and ticker tape. "What job?" he yelled. His face looked angry.

11 "The secretarial job," Pitcher said quietly. "You told me yesterday to call the school. I asked them to send one over this morning."

12 "You're losing your mind, Pitcher! Why would I tell you a thing like that? Miss Leslie has worked well for a whole year here. The job is hers while she wants to stay. There is no job here, Madam! Tell the secretarial school, Pitcher. Don't bring any more of them in here!"

13 The lady turned to leave. Her hat almost hit Pitcher in the eye as she angrily walked past him out of the office. Pitcher thought to himself that Maxwell was getting more forgetful every day.

II

14 The office became busier and busier. Orders to buy and sell came and went like birds flying. Maxwell was worried about his own stocks, too, and worked faster and harder. This was the stock market, the world of money. There was no room in it for the world of human feelings or the world of nature.

15 Near lunchtime, everything quieted down. Maxwell stood by his desk with his hands full of telegrams. His pen was behind his ear. His hair stood up on his head. Suddenly through the open window came a smell of flowers, like the thin breath of spring. Maxwell stood still. This was Miss Leslie's smell, her own and only hers. The smell seemed to bring her before him. The world of the stock market disappeared. And Miss Leslie was in the next room—only twenty steps away.

16 "I'll do it now," said Maxwell softly. "I'll ask her now. Why didn't I do it long ago?"

17 He ran into her office. He jumped towards her desk. She looked up at him with a smile. Her face turned a soft pink. Her eyes were kind. Maxwell put his hands on her desk. They were still full of papers.

18 "Miss Leslie," he said, hurrying, "I only have a moment to talk. I want to say something important in that moment: Will you be my wife? I haven't had time to show you, but I really do love you. Speak quickly please—there's the telephone."

19 "Why—what are you talking about?" cried the young lady. She stood up and looked at him strangely.

20 "Don't you understand?" Maxwell asked quickly, looking back at the phone on his desk. "I want you to marry me. I've stolen this moment to ask you, now, while things have quieted down a little. Take the telephone, Pitcher!" he yelled. "Will you, Miss Leslie?" he added softly.

21 The secretary acted very strange. At first she seemed surprised. Then she began to cry. But then she smiled through her tears like the sun through rain. She put

her arm around the stockbroker's neck.

22 "I know now," she said. "It's this business that put it out of your head. I was afraid, at first. But don't you remember, Harvey? We were married last evening at 8:00, in the little church around the corner."

THE ROMANCE OF A BUSY BROKER
EXERCISES

A. Understanding the Plot of the Story

Answer the following questions with complete sentences.

1. What is Maxwell's business?
2. Who works with him, and what do they do? In the picture on p.5, which man is Pitcher and which is Maxwell?
3. Why is Pitcher so interested in Maxwell this morning?
4. What telephone call did Pitcher make for Maxwell yesterday? Why?
5. What question does Maxwell ask Miss Leslie?
6. Why is she so surprised?

PART I (PAGES 4–6)
B. Close Reading: Determining the Facts

Below are some statements about Part I of "The Romance of a Busy Broker." If the statement is true, write "T" beside it. If it is not true, write "F" for false, and then write a sentence that is true.

1. ___ Pitcher was an energetic man, and his feelings could always be seen in his face.

2. ___ Harvey Maxwell was a man who put great energy into his work.

3. ___ The young lady with Maxwell seemed unhappy, and she dressed badly.

4. ___ The young lady asked Pitcher if Maxwell had asked him to get another secretary.

5. ___ The young lady went to her desk because no one from the secretarial school had arrived.

6. ___ The office was quiet and peaceful after Maxwell and the young lady began work.

7. ___ Maxwell told the young lady from the secretarial school that the job was hers if she wanted it.

C. Word Forms

Put the correct form of the word on the left in the blank spaces on the right.

1. (surprise/surprised) Pitcher, a quiet man, looked _____ this morning. The _____ for him was the arrival of Harvey Maxwell and his secretary together.

2. (interest/interested) Pitcher, _____ in the young lady's actions, watched her carefully. He noticed with _____ that she did not walk inside to her own desk as usual.

3. (crowds/crowded) The office seemed _____ with businessmen buying and selling, and boys running in and out with telegrams. These _____ came into the office every day.

4. (dress/dressed) The young lady's _____ was grey and plain and beautiful. Later, another woman came into the office, _____ brightly, with cheap jewelry and a large round hat.

5. (change/changed) _____ into a machine as soon as he entered his office, Maxwell dug into a mountain of letters and telegrams. The _____ in the man was complete: he no longer seemed like a man.

PART II (PAGES 7–8)

D. Vocabulary

The paragraph below tells what happened in Part II. Fill in the blanks with words that help tell the story. If you cannot think of a word that makes sense in one of the blanks, choose one from the list that follows the paragraph. But try first to fill in the blanks with words you already know.

After the lady from the secretarial school left, Maxwell became _____ . He was worried about his own _____, and worked _____ and _____. There was no room for human _____ in his world of money. But near lunchtime everything _____down. Maxwell smelled a smell of _____ through the window. It made him think of Miss Leslie. "I'll do it now," he thought, and went into her _____ . Miss Leslie _____ when she saw him. But Maxwell was in a _____ and spoke fast. "Will you _____ me?" he asked. She was angry at first, then she began to _____. But at last she smiled through her _____ . "I know now," she said. "It's this _____ that put it out of your head. We were last night at the little _____ around the corner."

marry	feelings	quieted	talking
flowers	tears	business	busier
office	stocks	smiled	faster
church	harder	married	cry
	hurry		

E. Language Activity: Following the New York Stock Exchange

Now, stockbrokers do not use ticker tape machines as they did in the old days. But the buying and selling of stocks has not changed very much. Businessmen and businesswomen still follow the stock "market" carefully. One way they do this is by reading about stocks every day in the newspaper. Here are some examples from the long list of stocks that are bought and sold on the New York Stock Exchange (or market).

NATIONWIDE NEW YORK STOCK EXCHANGE

1	2	3	4	5	6	7
52-Week			Current Week			
High	Low	Stock	High	Low	Last	Change
6 1/4	3 3/8	AcmeE	5 1/8	4 3/4	4 3/4	-1/8
80 5/8	54 3/8	Alcoa	74 1/4	71 7/8	72 3/4	-1/4
49 3/4	30 5/8	BankAm	44	40 1/4	41 1/2	-1 3/4
60 1/2	41 1/2	BauschL	50 3/4	48 1/8	50 3/8	+2 3/8
15	7 1/2	Ceridian	15	14	14 1/2	+1/2
32 3/4	20 3/4	ClubMed	23 3/4	23	23 1/4	-1/4
41 1/8	25 7/8	Disney	36 7/8	34	35 7/8	+1 3/8
4 3/8	3	DukeRt	4 1/8	4	4 1/8	+1/8

Columns 1 and 2 show the high and low price of the stock last year (52 weeks).

Column 3 shows the names of companies that offer stock for sale.

Columns 4 and 5 show the high and low price of the stock during the past week.

Column 6 shows the price of the stock at the end of the week.

Column 7 shows the change in the price of the stock during the past week.

Working alone, or with another student, try to find answers to the following questions from the list on page 12.

1. Which company above had the highest price during the current week? Which had the lowest?
2. Which company had the greatest positive change in its price last week? Which had the greatest negative change in price?
3. Which company had the greatest change in its price last year? Which had the smallest?
4. Which company would you like to own stock in: the Bank of America, Club Med, or Disney? Why?
5. Look at the stock listings in today's newspaper. Choose one or two stocks to "buy." Follow your stocks for a week or two. Discover whether you would have gained or lost money by buying that stock.

F. Writing: Controlled Composition
"The Romance of a Busy Broker"

Answer the following questions with complete sentences. Make a paragraph of your answers. You will have a summary of "The Romance of a Busy Broker." Make sure you include in your answers the words that are underlined in the questions.

1. Where did Pitcher work?
2. What kind of man was he usually?
3. But how did he act this morning?
4. Why was he interested this morning?
5. How did Maxwell usually arrive at the office?
6. What did Maxwell do after he said "Good morning"?
7. What did Miss Leslie ask Pitcher?
8. Then what did she do?
9. As the morning passed, how did the office seem, and how did Maxwell act?
10. Who came into the office then?
11. Why had she come?

   12. What did Maxwell say to her?

   13. How did she feel? <u>And</u> what did she do?

   14. <u>Later</u>, <u>near lunch time</u>, what happened in the office?

   15. What did Maxwell <u>suddenly</u> smell?

   16. What did the smell make Maxwell think of?

   17. What did he decide to do?

   18. <u>When</u> he went into Miss Leslie's office, what did he say?

   19. <u>At first</u>, how did she act?

   20. What did she understand <u>later</u>?

   21. What had the busy broker forgotten?

G. Discussion: How Busy Can Busy Get?

   1. Can you remember a time when you were so busy that you forgot something important? What were you doing? What did you forget?

   2. Can you remember a time when someone else was so busy that he or she forgot something important about *you*? What was it? How did you feel? What did you do?

   3. In "The Romance of a Busy Broker," Harvey Maxwell is so busy that he forgets that he was married "last evening at 8:00, in the little church around the corner." Do you believe this is possible? If so, and if you were the woman, would you act the way Miss Leslie did? If you don't believe it, did you enjoy the story anyway? Why, or why not?

Notes:

_____

_____

_____

_____

THE BRIDE COMES TO YELLOW SKY

Before You Read the Story ...

1. *A Life*

Read the paragraph about Stephen Crane on page 17. Do you expect that the characters in this story will be rich city people? Why or why not? In what part of the country do you expect the story to take place?

2. *The Pictures*

Look at the picture on page 19. Where do you think the people are sitting? Why do you think so? Now read the first sentence of the story. Did you guess correctly?

3. *Thinking About It ...*

Look at the title of the story. Yellow Sky is the name of a small town. Who is coming there? What do you imagine when you think of the word "bride?" Does the picture on page 25 match the ideas you have of what a new bride might expect? Why or why not? Are unexpected experiences frightening or funny to you? Why?

4. *Scanning to Find Numbers, Dates, or Key Words*

Read the questions below. For each question, scan the paragraph about Stephen Crane on page 17. Look for the number, date, key word, or phrase underlined in the question. Try to answer all five questions in less than two minutes.

a. What happened to Crane in <u>1871</u>?

b. What was <u>"Maggie: A Girl of the Streets"</u>?

c. What happened when Crane was <u>24</u>?

d. What happened to Crane in <u>1896</u>?

e. What happened when Crane was <u>29</u>?

THE BRIDE COMES TO YELLOW SKY

adapted from the story by
STEPHEN CRANE

Stephen Crane was born in 1871 in New Jersey. He studied at Lafayette College and at Syracuse University. After college he worked for several newspapers in New York City. His first story, "Maggie: A Girl of the Streets," is about life among poor people of the city. He became famous suddenly at 24 when he wrote The Red Badge of Courage. It is a realistic story about a young, frightened soldier in the U.S. Civil War. In 1896 Crane was sent by his newspaper to the Western United States and to Mexico. He had many exciting adventures with cowboys and criminals. Many of his best stories, like "The Bride Comes to Yellow Sky," were written during this time. Crane died in 1900. He was only 29, but he had written twelve volumes of novels, stories, and poems.

I

The great express train was speeding westward across Texas. Outside the window the plains stretched towards the horizon. There were vast areas of green grassland, large areas of desert, and occasional houses and trees.

2 A newly married couple had boarded the train at San Antonio. The man, Jack Potter, was wearing new black clothes. His face and hands were red from many days in the wind and sun. Sitting with a red hand on each knee, he looked shyly at the other passengers. From time to time he rearranged his new clothes.

3 The bride was neither very pretty nor very young. Her blue dress was decorated with a little velvet, and many steel buttons. Her fashionable clothes made her feel uncomfortable. Twisting her head, she often examined her large velvet sleeves. Her plain face turned red when the other passengers glanced at her.

4 The couple seemed to be very happy. "Ever been on a train before?" he asked. His face shone with delight.

5 "No," she answered. "I never have. It's fine, isn't it?"

6 "Great! And soon we'll go forward to the dining coach and eat. Finest meal in the world! Costs a dollar."

7 "Oh, does it?" cried the bride. "Costs a dollar? That's too much for us, isn't it, Jack?"

8 "Not this trip," he answered bravely.

9 Later he explained to her about the trains.

10 "You see, it's a thousand miles from one end of Texas to the other; and this train runs straight across and only stops four times." He had the pride of an owner. He

pointed out to her the rich decoration of the coach. Her eyes opened wide as she looked at the sea-green velvet, the glowing wood, and the shining brass, silver, and glass. In the minds of the couple, their rich surroundings shone with the glory of their new marriage. The man's face glowed with pride and delight.

11 Yet he looked foolish to the Negro porter who glanced at them from a distance. The porter bullied them when he served them, but he did not make it obvious that he was bullying them. The other passengers smiled. Historically, there was supposed to be something funny in their situation.

12 "We are due in Yellow Sky at 3:42," he said, looking tenderly into her eyes.

13 "Oh, are we?" she said, as if surprised. She took from her pocket a little silver watch, and as she held it in front of her, the new husband's face shone.

14 "I bought it in San Antonio from a friend of mine," he told her happily.

15 "It's seventeen minutes past twelve," she said, looking up at him tenderly.

16 A passenger, seeing her expression, raised an eyebrow.

17 Later they went to the dining car. Two rows of waiters in white suits watched with interest as they entered. The waiter who served them guided them through the meal in a fatherly way. And yet, as they returned to their coach, their faces showed a look of relief.

18 Out of the window, down a long purple slope, the Rio Grande River twisted. The town of Yellow Sky was beside it. As the train approached its destination, the husband became more and more nervous. His red fingers tapped his knees. He seemed to be thinking about something else, when the bride leaned forward to speak to him.

19 He had begun to worry that he had not let the community know about his marriage. As the marshal, he was an important person in town. He could not deny the importance of his marriage to the community. Only the fire

in the new hotel could equal it. He knew his friends would not forgive him for not consulting them. He had almost sent a telegram but he had decided instead on secrecy.

20 As the train approached town, the marshal felt a new fear. The citizens had a brass band that played badly. If they knew of his plans, they would march him and his new wife with cheers and laughter from the train station to his house.

21 To avoid the community, he decided to make the trip from the station to his house as quickly as possible. When they were safe at home, he would announce his marriage. Then he would stay home until the town's excitement disappeared.

22 The bride looked anxiously at him. "What's worrying you, Jack?"

23 He laughed nervously. "I'm not worrying, girl. I'm only thinking of Yellow Sky."

24 They looked at each other softly, but Potter continued to laugh the same nervous laugh.

25 "We're nearly there," he said.

26 Presently, the porter came to announce the stop. He brushed off Potter's new clothes, then took their bag. The two engines with the long string of coaches rushed into the station of Yellow Sky.

27 "They have to take water here," Potter said, like someone announcing a death. Before the train stopped, he was relieved to see that the station platform was completely empty except for the station agent. When the train stopped, the porter got down and lowered a little step.

28 "Come on, girl," said Potter. As he helped her down, they each laughed nervously. He took the bag from the porter and gave his wife his arm. At a distance the station agent started waving his arms towards them. Potter gripped his wife's arm firmly to his side, and they hurried away. Behind him the porter laughed.

II

29 The California express train was due in Yellow Sky in twenty-one minutes. There were six men at the Tired

Traveller Bar. One was a stranger who talked constantly. Three were Texans who did not care to talk at that time. Two were Mexicans who talked infrequently when they were at the Tired Traveller. The barkeeper's dog lay outside in front of the door. His head resting on his paws, he glanced here and there with the attitude of an animal that is often bullied.

30 Except for the stranger and his companions in the bar, Yellow Sky was asleep. The stranger was leaning on the bar telling a story when a young man suddenly appeared. He shouted, "Scratchy Wilson's been drinking! There'll be some shooting!" The two Mexicans at once put down their glasses and went out by the back door of the bar. The others became silent.

31 "Say, what is this?" asked the stranger.

32 "It means, my friend," answered the youth, "for the next two hours this town will not be very safe."

33 The barkeeper went to the door and locked it. He went to the windows and pulled down heavy boards across them. The room became dark, and the stranger looked from one to another.

34 "But say," he cried, "What is this, anyhow? Is there going to be a gunfight?"

35 "Don't know if there'll be a fight or not," answered one man. "but there'll be some good shooting."

36 "Oh, there'll be a fight fast enough if anyone wants one," said the youth. "Anybody can get a fight out there in the street. There's a fight just waiting."

37 The stranger looked worried.

38 "What did you say his name was?" he asked.

39 "Scratchy Wilson," they all answered together.

40 "And will he kill anybody? What are you going to do? Does this happen often? How often does this happen? Can he break down that door?"

41 "No, he can't break down the door," replied the barkeeper. "He's tried it three times. But when he comes, you'd better lie down on the floor, stranger. He's sure to shoot at the door, and a bullet may come through."

42 The stranger kept an eye on the door now. "Will he

kill anybody?" he said again.

43 The others laughed at the question.

44 "He's going to shoot. It's best to keep away from him."

45 "But what do you do in a case like this? What do you do?"

46 A man answered, "Why, he and Jack Potter—"

47 "But," the others all said, "Jack Potter is in San Antonio."

48 "Well, what's he got to do with it?"

49 "Oh, he's the town marshal. He goes out and fights Scratchy."

50 "Wow!" said the stranger, "nice job he's got."

51 The stranger wanted to ask more questions but the others motioned him to stay silent. A tense silence hung over them. In the dark shadows of the room their eyes shone as they listened to sounds from the street. One man motioned to the barkeeper, who handed him a bottle and a glass. The man poured a full glass of whiskey and put down the bottle quietly. He swallowed and turned silently toward the door. The stranger saw that the barkeeper, without a sound, had taken a gun from under the bar.

52 "You better come behind the bar with me," the barkeeper whispered to him.

53 The stranger took a seat on a box with his head below the top of the bar.

54 The barkeeper sat on a nearby box. "You see," he whispered, "this Scratchy is a terror with a gun. When he goes on the wartrail we head for our holes—naturally. He's terrible when he's been drinking. Otherwise he's all right—kind of simple—wouldn't hurt a fly—nicest fellow in town. But when he's drunk—whoo!"

55 There was a period of silence. "I wish Jack Potter was back from San Antonio," said the barkeeper. "He shot Wilson once—in the leg—and he would take care of this situation."

56 Presently they heard from a distance the sound of a shot, then the sound of three wild shouts. The men in the dark bar looked at each other. "Here he comes," they said.

III

57 A man turned a corner and walked into the middle of the main street of Yellow Sky. In each hand he held a long, heavy, blue-black revolver. Often he shouted, and these furious cries rang through the town. The man's face was red with whiskey. His eyes hunted the doorways and windows. He walked with the creeping movement of a cat, shouting fierce challenges into the silence. The long revolvers in his hands were ready for action.

58 No one answered his challenge. No one offered a fight.

59 The barkeeper's dog lay sleeping in front of his master's door. At the sight of the dog, the man paused and raised his revolver humorously. At the sight of the man, the dog sprang up and started to walk away. The man shouted, and the dog started to run. As the dog was about to turn a corner, there was a loud noise, a whistling, and a bullet hit the ground just in front of it. The dog screamed, turned, and headed in a new direction. Again there was a noise, a whistling, and sand was kicked up violently in front of it. Terrified, the dog turned and shrank back like an animal in a cage. The man stood laughing, his weapons ready.

60 Finally the man was attracted to the Tired Traveller Bar. He went to the door, hammered it with a revolver, and demanded a drink.

61 The door stayed closed. He picked up a piece of paper from the ground and attached it to the door with a knife. Then he turned his back in disgust and walked to the opposite side of the street. Turning quickly on his heel, he fired at the piece of paper. He missed it by a half-inch. He swore at himself and went away. Later he shot out the windows of his closest friend's house. The man was playing with the town. It was a toy to him.

62 But still no one offered to fight him. He thought of Jack Potter, his old enemy, and decided to go to Potter's house and force him to fight. When he arrived at Potter's house, it was silent, like the rest of the town.

63 Standing in front of the house, the man shouted a challenge. But the house was as silent as a great stone god. It gave no sign. After a short wait, the man screamed other challenges. The house remained silent. Screaming with rage, the man began to shoot. He only paused for breath and to reload his revolvers.

IV

64 Potter and his bride walked quickly as if they were bowed against a strong wind. Sometimes they laughed together quietly.

65 "Next corner, dear," he said finally.

66 Potter started to raise a finger to point out their new home. But as they turned the corner, they came face to face with a man furiously pushing bullets into a large revolver. Instantly the man dropped the revolver to the ground and pulled out another. This revolver was aimed at the bridegroom's chest.

67 There was a silence. Potter loosened his arm from the woman's grip and dropped the bag to the ground. The bride looked terrified. Her face turned as yellow as an old cloth.

68 The two men faced each other. The one with the revolver smiled with quiet fury.

69 "You tried to surprise me," he said fiercely. "Tried to surprise me!"

70 As Potter made a slight movement, the man moved his revolver closer to the marshal's chest. "No, don't you do it, Jack Potter. Don't you move a finger toward a gun. Don't move an eyelash. The time has come for us to settle accounts."

71 Potter looked at his enemy. "I don't have a gun on me, Scratchy," he said, trying to calm the man. "Honest, I don't." He was steady. Somewhere in the back of his mind was a vision of the train coach: the sea-green velvet, the shining brass, silver, and glass—all the glory of his new marriage. "You know I fight when it's time to fight, Scratchy, but I don't have a gun on me. You'll have to do all

the shooting yourself."

72 His enemy's face grew furious. He stepped forward and moved his weapon back and forth in front of Potter's chest. "Don't tell me you don't have a gun. Nobody in Texas has ever seen you without a gun." His eyes blazed with light, and his throat worked like a pump.

73 Potter had not retreated an inch. "I tell you I don't have a gun, and I don't," answered Potter. "If you're going to shoot me, you better begin now. You'll never get a chance like this again."

74 Wilson grew calmer. "If you don't have gun, why don't you?" he said. "Been to church?"

75 "I don't have a gun because I've just arrived from San Antonio with my wife. I'm married," said Potter. "If I had known there would be trouble, I'd have a gun, and don't you forget it."

76 "Married!" said Scratchy, not understanding.

77 "Yes, married. I'm married," said Potter, distinctly.

78 "Married?" said Scratchy. For the first time, he saw the frightened woman standing next to the marshal.

79 "No!" he said. He was like a creature who has seen another world. He stepped backward, and his arm with the revolver fell to his side. "Is this the lady?" he asked.

80 "Yes, this is the lady," answered Potter.

81 There was another period of silence.

82 "Well," said Wilson at last, slowly. "I suppose the fight's off now."

83 "It's off if you say so, Scratchy. You know I didn't start the trouble." Potter lifted his bag.

84 "Well, I say it's off, Jack," said Wilson. He was looking at the ground. "Married!" He was a simple child of the Old West in the presence of this foreign condition. He picked up his dropped revolver and walked away. His feet made long, deep marks in the heavy sand.

THE BRIDE COMES TO YELLOW SKY
EXERCISES

A. Understanding the Plot of the Story

Answer the following questions with complete sentences.

1. Where, and how, are Jack Potter and his wife travelling?
2. How does Potter act as they approach Yellow Sky? Why?
3. What news does the young man bring to the men in the Tired Traveller Bar?
4. Why does Scratchy Wilson begin shooting? What do the townspeople do?
5. What does Scratchy expect Jack Potter to do when they meet?
6. Why doesn't Potter have his gun with him?
7. What news does Potter tell Scratchy, and how does Scratchy react.

PART I (PAGES 18–21)

B. Close Reading: Understanding Feelings from Actions

Below, you will read some sentences from Part I of the story. Each sentence describes an action that happens in the story. The author wants this action to suggest something about his character's feelings. After each sentence you will find three sentences that describe how the character might have felt. Choose sentence a, b, or c, and tell what other words or phrases in the story helped you make your choice. A paragraph number is given so that you can find the sentence in the story.

1. "From time to time he rearranged his new clothes." (paragraph 2)
   a. He was unhappy because his new clothes didn't fit him.
   b. He was a man from the country, and he felt uncomfortable wearing new clothes like these.
   c. He dressed carefully, and he enjoyed rearranging his clothes to look perfect.

`What other words or phrases in the paragraph helped you choose **a**, **b**, or **c** above? _____

2. "He pointed out to her the rich decoration of the coach." (paragraph 10)

   a. He wanted to be sure she had noticed how beautiful the coach was.

   b. He felt uncomfortable surrounded by such rich decoration, and he wanted to show her why.

   c. He was very proud of the decoration of the coach, and felt it was a kind of gift from him to her.

What other words or phrases in the paragraph helped you choose **a**, **b**, or **c** above? _____

3. "The other passengers smiled." (paragraph 11)

   a. They thought the newly married couple seemed rather foolish, and rather funny.

   b. They were pleased to see such a nice example of young love.

   c. They smiled because they, too, were pleased with the richly decorated train.

What other word or phrases in the paragraph helped you choose **a**, **b**, or **c** above? _____

4. "And yet, as they returned to their coach, their faces showed a look of relief." (paragraph 17)

   a. They hadn't liked their waiter because he was rude to them.

   b. It had made them nervous to eat an expensive meal in a strange place.

   c. The cheap (one dollar) meal had not been very good, and they were happy to get away.

What other words or phrases in the paragraph helped you choose **a**, **b**, or **c** above? _____

5. "'They have to take water here,' Potter said, like someone announcing a death." (paragraph 27)

   a. He was worried because he hadn't told the people
   of his town about his marriage. So, everything he
   said sounded sad or gloomy.

   b. He was worried because it would take time to take
   on the water, and he wanted to get home as fast as
   possible.

   c. He was sad because their marriage trip was ending,
   and their daily, unexciting married life was about to
   begin.

   What other words or phrases in the paragraph helped

   you choose **a**, **b**, or **c** above?_____

C. Word Forms

For each group of sentences below, fill in the blanks with
the correct forms of the words given.

1. uncomfortable, uncomfortably

   a. The man's clothes felt _____ .

   b. He looked _____ at his clothes.

2. rough, roughly, roughness

   a. Sun and wind had made his skin red and _____.

   b. Work and weather had caused the _____ of

   his hands.

   c. He never spoke _____ to his bride.

3. shy, shyly, shyness

   a. Her _____ was clear to everyone, for she

   never lifted her eyes.

   b. They felt _____ when others looked at

   them.

   c. The man looked _____ at his new bride.

4. embarrassment, embarrassed, embarrassing

   a. They tried not to be _____ by the passengers' smiles.

   b. His _____ showed on his face, which was pinker than usual.

   c. It is _____ to make a mistake in public.

5. fool, foolish, foolishly

   a. The passengers smiled because they thought the coupled looked _____.

   b. The couple smiled _____ because they were embarrassed.

   c. The porter made Jack Potter feel like a _____.

6. secret, secrecy, secretly

   a. In the matter of telling the town about his marriage, the marshal had decided on _____.

   b. He wanted his marriage to remain _____.

   c. They had been married _____ in another part of the state.

PART II (PAGES 21–23)

D. Vocabulary

The following pairs of words are *antonyms*, or opposites. Choose the pair of antonyms that best completes the meaning of each sentence below.

whispered–shouted	safe–dangerous
constantly–infrequently	sober–drunk

1. Scratchy is wild only when he's _____; he wouldn't hurt a fly when he's _____.

2. As soon as a young man _____ the news of Scratchy's arrival, the men inside the bar _____ to each other.

3. Clearly, Scratchy is a _____ man when he's been drinking; no one is _____ around him.

4. Only the stranger in Yellow Sky talked _____; the men who lived there talked _____, or not all.

Here are three more vocabulary words from Part II. Make your own sentence using each one. Then think of an antonym for each vocabulary word. Use a dictionary, if necessary. Then use each of the antonyms in a new sentence.

5. appear (paragraph 30: "... a young man suddenly appeared.")

_____

_____

6. tense (paragraph 51: "A tense silence hung over them.")

_____

_____

7. simple (paragraph 54: "Otherwise he's all right—kind of simpl ...")

_____

_____

PART III (PAGES 24–27)

E. Close Reading: Scratchy on the Wartrail

Part III is a short section that introduces us to Scratchy

Wilson (who is usually "all right—kind of simple— wouldn't hurt a fly—nicest fellow in town"). In the exercise below, join the beginning of a sentence in column A to its logical ending from column B. Check back to Part III to make sure that your sentences give an accurate picture of Scratchy.

A	B
1. He shouted challenges as his eyes	a. to put more bullets in his gun.
2. He stood there laughing	b. missed the piece of paper.
3. He hit the saloon door with his gun, then	c. hunted the doorways and windows of the empty town.
4. He swore at himself because he	
5. He thought that if he shot at Potter's house	d. at the terror of the dog.
	e. called for a drink.
6. He stopped screaming only	f. Potter would come out to fight.

PART IV (PAGES 26–27)

F. Language Activity: Understanding Irony of Situation

(If possible, work on this exercise with another student or in a group of three to four students.)

When we say that a situation is ironic, we meant that, in a humorous way, it is the opposite of what we expected. The situation at the end of "The Bride Comes to Yellow Sky" is full of irony. Below are three quotations from ironic moments in the story. Each quotation is followed by questions which will help you explore the irony of that moment. Discuss these questions with your partner(s) and then, in your own words, tell what is ironic about the particular scene or moment you have discussed.

1. "Potter and his bride walked quickly as if they were bowed against a strong wind."

   a. Why are they walking bent over ("as if bowed against a strong wind")?

     b. Why are they walking quickly?

     c. How would you expect a newly married couple to look, walking toward their new house?

     d. What is the marshal afraid of? And how would you expect a marshal to enter his own town?

     e. At this moment, is the marshal probably more afraid of meeting his townspeople, or Scratchy Wilson?

     f. Whom does the marshal expect to meet? Whom does he actually meet?

2. "Don't move an eyelash. The time has come for us to settle accounts."

Scratchy is ready for a fight. Here we have a famous gunfight scene from the Old West: a marshal and a bad man, facing each other on a street in a Texas town. But isn't the story's situation different from what we might expect?

     a. There is an extra person in the scene. Who is it? What effect does this person have on the two men?

     b. What about weapons? What are Scratchy's weapons? What are the marshal's? What effect does this have on the fight?

3. "He was like a creature who has seen another world."

     a. What is Scratchy so surprised about?

     b. What can't he understand?

     c. In the past, what made peace between the marshal and Scratchy?

     d. What makes peace this time?

G. Writing: Controlled Composition
"Conclusion of Yellow Sky"

Answer each pair of questions below. Then put your two answers into one sentence, using the connector given in parentheses. The first one is done for you as an example. When you have eight sentences (including the sample), put them together in a paragraph. You will have a summary of the end of "The Bride Comes to Yellow Sky."

1. Did Jack Potter and his bride walk toward Jack's house or toward the saloon? Had they gotten off the train, or had they walked all the way across Texas? (*after*) <u>Jack Potter and his bride walked toward Jack's house after they had gotten off the train.</u>

2. Who was in front of the house? What was he doing? (*and*)

3. Had Scratchy been drinking, or not? Did he want to fight Potter, or did he want to continue drinking? (*and now*)

4. Did Potter tell him that he always fought when he had to, or did he remain silent? Did he take out a gun, or did he say that he didn't have a gun at the moment? (*but*)

5. Did Scratchy believe him, or not? Had Potter never been seen without a bride, or without a gun? (*because*)

6. Did Potter tell Scratchy that he was married, or that he was angry? Whom did Scratchy seem to notice for the first time? (*when*)

7. Was there silence for a moment, or a sudden shout? Did Scratchy step backward and lower his gun, or did he step forward and try to shoot Potter? (*and then*)

8. What was beyond his understanding? Did he take his guns and walk away, or did he warmly welcome the bride to town? (*so*)

H. Discussion: A Sense of Humor

1. Stephen Crane's intention in "The Bride Comes to Yellow Sky" was to write a story that was humorous in an ironic way. Do you think he succeeded—that is, did you find the story humorous? funny? Did it make you laugh? smile? Can you say why?

2. Compare "The Bride Comes to Yellow Sky" and "The Romance of a Busy Broker." Which story, in your opinion, is funnier? Which is more "real"? Which has the more believable characters? Which did you like better? Can you say why?

3. Can you think of a movie, TV show, story, or book that has made you laugh out loud? What was it? Can you explain why you found it funny? In general, what type of humor do you prefer?

THE CASK OF AMONTILLADO

Before You Read the Story ...

1. *A Life*

Read the paragraph about Edgar Allan Poe on page 37. Would you expect Poe's tales to be realistic or imaginative? Why?

2. *The Picture*

Look at the picture on page 42. Where are the two men in the picture? What makes you think so? How are the men dressed? Why do you think they are dressed that way? What seems to be happening in the picture?

3. *Thinking About It ...*

A *cask* is a large barrel which, usually, contains wine. *Amontillado* (pronounced Ah-mon-tee-YAH-doe) is a type of wine called *sherry*. The most famous Amontillado comes from Spain. Yet we cannot be sure that the story, "The Cask of Amontillado," is set in Spain. Certainly it is set in a country which, like Spain or Italy, has a *Carnival* season. This is a period of feasting and merry-making before a period of strict religious observance. Many non-Christian as well as Christian cultures have a period like that of Carnival. Does yours? What happens during that period?

4. *Scanning for General Information*

Sometimes we *scan* a piece of writing not to look for specific information or facts, but to learn as much as we can about a more general topic.

In this exercise, you are asked to find information about Edgar Allan Poe's *work* and *writing*. You want to know about the kinds of work Poe did during his life, and you want to learn about the kind of writing he did. For this exercise, nothing else about Poe is very important to you.

Read the paragraph about Poe on page 37. Take no more than two minutes to read it. Remember to look for information about his work and writing. After you have read the paragraph, read and mark the statements below either "T" for true or "F" for false. How many of them can you get correct after one reading of the paragraph? after two?

a. _____ Poe worked as an actor when he was young.

b. _____ Poe worked for some literary magazines as an editor.

c. _____ Poe often lost his job.

d. _____ Poe is best known for his long novels.

e. _____ Poe wrote poetry and stories, not just stories.

f. _____ Most of Poe's stories are humorous and have surprise endings.

g. _____ Poe wrote mystery and detective stories, not horror stories.

THE CASK OF AMONTILLADO

adapted from the story by
EDGAR ALLAN POE

Edgar Allan Poe was born in 1809 in Boston, Massachusetts. His parents died when he was a child, and he was brought up by a wealthy couple, John and Frances Allan, in Richmond, Virginia. He quarreled with the Allans when he was a young man, and left home. He worked as an editor for several literary magazines, but lost his job frequently because he drank too much. His own writing—poetry and short stories—became increasingly popular, but he remained poor in spite of his literary success. He died in 1849. Poe is generally considered the first writer of mystery or detective stories. "The Murders of the Rue Morgue" and "The Gold Bug" are among these. He is equally famous for the horror stories—such as "The Tell-Tale Heart," "The Fall of the House of Usher," and "The Cask of Amontillado"—in which he explores the dark side of the human mind and heart.

I

I had borne the thousand injuries of Fortunato[1] as well as I could, but when he dared to insult me, I knew I must have revenge.

2 However, you, my friend, will understand that I never spoke a threat. I, Montressor,[2] would have revenge eventually; there was no doubt about that. But I wanted no risk. I wanted to punish, but to punish in safety, and with confidence. The insult would be paid back, yes. But also the insulter must know the punisher. And Montressor, the punisher, must go free.

3 I continued, therefore, to smile in Fortunato's face, as always. He could not know that my smile *now* was at the thought of his destruction.

4 He had a weakness, this Fortunato. He was proud of his knowledge of wines. In fact, he did know the old Italian wines very well—as I did. And this was excellent for my purposes.

5 It was about dusk, one evening during Carnival, when I found him walking along the crowded street. He greeted me with unusual warmth, for he had been drinking much. The man wore carnival clothes: a brightly colored shirt, tight pants, and a hat with little bells on it. I was so pleased to see him that I almost forgot to let go of his hand.

6 "My dear Fortunato," I said, "how well you look! But what do you think? I have received a cask of the real Amontillado[3] wine. At least they *say* it's the real thing. But I have my doubts."

7 "What, Montressor?" said he. "Amontillado? A whole cask? Impossible! And in the middle of Carnival!"

1 Pronounced: For-tune-*AH* toe
2 Mon-tress-*SORE*
3 Ah-mon-tee-*YAH*-doe

8 "I have my doubts," I repeated. "And do you know, I was foolish enough to pay the full Amontillado price. I had to do it without asking you. I couldn't find you, and I didn't want to lose a bargain."

9 "Amontillado!"

10 "I have my doubts."

11 "Amontillado!"

12 "And I must bury them."

13 "Amontillado!"

14 "Since you are busy, I am going to find Luchresi.[4] If anyone has the ability to judge, it is he. He will tell me—"

15 "Luchresi cannot tell the difference between Amontillado and ordinary wine."

16 "And yet some fools say that his taste is equal to yours."

17 "Come, let us go."

18 "Where?"

19 "To your vaults."

20 "My friend, no. I refuse to give you trouble in this way. I see that you are on your way to a party. Luchresi—"

21 "I am going nowhere. Come."

22 "My friend, no. It is not only the party. I see you have a bad cold. My vaults are terribly damp. You will suffer."

23 "Let us go anyway. My cold is nothing. And Luchresi? I tell you, the man cannot tell Amontillado from milk!"

24 Speaking in this way, Fortunato took my arm. Putting on a mask of black silk in order to mix with the Carnival crowd, I allow him to hurry me to my palazzo.[5]

25 There were no servants at home; they were all enjoying the Carnival. I had told them that I would not return to the palazzo until the morning. To them, this announcement was like an invitation to go on vacation.

26 I took two torches from their holders. Giving one to Fortunato, I led him through many rooms. We came to the door that led into the vaults. We walked through it and

4 Loo-*CRAY*-zee
5 Pah-*LAHT*-so

down a long and winding staircase. I requested him continuously to be careful. At last we came to the bottom and stood on the damp ground of the burial vaults of my family, the Montressors.

II

27 The footsteps of my friend were unsteady, and the bells on his hat lightly rang as he walked.

28 "The cask?" said he.

29 "It is a little further," I said. "But look at the white mold on the walls down here."

30 He turned towards me unsteadily. I saw in his eyes how much he had been drinking.

31 "What did you say?" he asked.

32 "Mold," I repeated, "the mold on the walls. How long have you had that bad cough?"

33 "Ugh! ugh! ugh!—ugh! ugh! ugh!—ugh! ugh! ugh! ugh! ugh!—ugh! ugh! ugh!"

34 My poor friend could not reply for many minutes.

35 "It is nothing," he said at last.

36 "Come," I said with decision, "we will go back. Your health is precious. You are rich, admired, loved. You are happy, as I once was. You are a man who would be missed. For me, it is no matter. We will go back; you will be ill, and I cannot be responsible. Besides, there is Luchresi—"

37 "Enough!" he said. "The cough is a mere nothing; it will not kill me. I shall not die of a cough."

38 "True, true," I replied. "And indeed I did not mean to frighten you. But you must use proper caution. A drink of this fine Medoc wine will protect us from the dampness."

39 Here, I broke off the neck of a bottle which I took from a long row that lay on the mold.

40 "Drink," I said, giving him the wine.

41 He raised it to his lips with a smile that I did not like.

42 He said, "I drink to the members of your fine family who are buried in these vaults."

43 "And I drink to your long life," I quietly replied. Again he took my arm and we continued. The wine shone

in his eyes. My own face was warm with the Medoc. We were deeper into the vaults now, and began to pass piles of human bones. I took Fortunato by an arm above the elbow.

44 "Look! The mold," I said. "See, it increases. It hangs from the roof of the vault. We must be below the river. That is why the dampness is so bad. Come, we will go back before it is too late. Your cough—"

45 "It is nothing," he said; "let us continue. But first another drink of the Medoc." He finished the wine in one swallow. Then he threw the bottle into the air with a strange motion that I did not understand. He repeated the motion again. His eyes questioned me, but I could only look at him in surprise.

46 "You do not understand the sign?" he said.

47 "No," I replied.

48 "Then you are not a Mason."

49 "A mason?" I said. "Isn't a mason someone who builds walls?"

50 "Ha! I mean a member of our secret society. We are called Masons. Have you never heard of us and our secret meetings?"

51 "Ah, yes, a mason," I said. "I am indeed a mason."

52 "You? Impossible! A Mason?"

53 "A real mason," I replied.

54 "Prove it," said he. "Give me the secret sign!"

55 "It is this," I answered. From a large pocket inside my coat I took a small tool. It was a trowel, used by masons to put plaster between the bricks in a wall.

56 "Ha! ha! You joke," he said. "Excellent! Now come. Let us continue to the Amontillado."

57 "Indeed," I said, and offered him my arm again. He leaned on it heavily. We passed through more rooms of bottles, casks, and bones. We went down one more staircase and arrived at last in the deepest room of the vaults. Here the human bones were piled as high as the ceiling. It was very dark, and our torches glowed rather weakly. At the far end of the large room there was still another, smaller room. It lay beyond an opening of one meter in width.

58 "Continue," I said. "The Amontillado is in there. I

wonder whether Luchresi—"

59 "He is a fool," my friend said as he stepped unsteadily forward into the last small room. I followed quickly after him. His progress was stopped by the bare wall ahead of him, which he looked at stupidly in confusion. In a moment I had chained him to the rock. On its surface were two iron rings, about two feet apart. A short chain hung from one of these rings, and a lock from the other. Throwing the chain quickly twice around his waist, I took only a few seconds to attach it to the lock. He was too astonished to struggle against me. Taking the key of the lock with me, I stepped back from the small room.

60 "If you place your hand on the wall," I said, "you will feel the mold. Indeed it is *very* damp. Once more I *beg* you to return with me. No? Then I must leave you. But first I should try to make you as comfortable as possible."

61 "The Amontillado!" cried my friend. He was not yet recovered from his astonishment.

62 "True," I replied; "the Amontillado."

63 As I said these words, I walked to the nearest small pile of bones. I began moving aside those on the top. Soon I uncovered some plaster and building stone. With these materials and with the help of my trowel, I began energetically to wall up the entrance to the small room.

64 I had laid only the first row of stones when I discovered that the effects of Fortunato's drinking had disappeared. The first sign of this was a low continual groan from the small room. It was not simply the groan of a man who has been drinking too much. Then there was a long and insistent silence. I laid the second row, and the third, and the fourth. And then I heard a furious shaking of the chains. I sat down and listened to it with satisfaction until it stopped. Then I finished the fifth, the sixth, and the seventh row. The wall was now at the height of my chest. I again paused, and holding my torch above the wall, I threw the light on the figure inside.

65 Loud, terrible screams burst from the throat of that chained form. They seemed to push me violently backward. For a brief moment I hesitated. But when I placed my hand

on the strong walls of the vault, I again felt satisfied. I approached the wall a second time. I replied to the screams with screams of my own. I echoed and reechoed the man, passing him in loudness and strength. I did this, and the screaming stopped.

66 My work was almost finished. I had completed the eighth, the ninth, and the tenth row. I had finished the eleventh, except for the final stone. I struggled with its weight; I had it almost into position. But now a low laugh came from the small room—a laugh that horrified me. It was followed by a sad voice, which I had difficulty recognizing as the voice of the noble Fortunato. The voice said—

67 "Ha! ha! ha!-he! he! he!—a very good joke indeed—an excellent joke! We will have much laughter about it at the palazzo—he! he! he!—over our wine!—he! he! he!"

68 "The Amontillado," I said.

69 "He! he! he!—he! he! he!—yes, the Amontillado. But it is getting late. Won't they be waiting for us at the palazzo, the Lady Fortunato and the rest? Let us be gone."

70 "Yes," I said, "let us be gone."

71 "Why? Why? For the love of God, Montressor! You're mad!"

72 "Yes," I said, "for the love of God!"

73 But there was no reply to these words. I waited. I called—

74 "Fortunato!"

75 No answer. I called again—

76 "Fortunato!"

77 No answer still. I placed a torch through the last hole and let is fall inside. Only a small ringing of bells came in return. My heart grew sick; it was the dampness of the vault. I hurried now in finishing. I forced the last stone into its position; I plastered it. I put the pile of old bones in front of the new wall. And for half a century, no man has disturbed them.

In pace requiescat! [6]

---

6 *In pace requiescat:* Latin for "May he rest in peace."

THE CASK OF AMONTILLADO
EXERCISES

A. Understanding the Plot of the Story

Answer the following questions with complete sentences.
1. Does Montressor like Fortunato? Why or why not?
2. What holiday is it when the two men meet?
3. What gift does Montressor tell Fortunato he has received?
4. What does Montressor tell Fortunato about the wine?
5. Where do the two men go, and why?
6. What sign does Fortunato give Montressor? What does Montressor take from his pocket?
7. What does Montressor do to Fortunato when they reach the last room underground?

PART I (PAGES 38–40)

B. Close Reading: Understanding Key Ideas and Relationships

Below are some sentences from Part I of "The Cask of Amontillado." After each sentence are questions which refer to certain words or phrases in the sentence and test your understanding of the ideas or relationships introduced in the sentence. A paragraph number is given to help you locate the sentence in the text of the story.

1. "But also the insulter must know the punisher " (paragraph 2)

    a. The "insulter" here is _____.

    b. The "punisher" is _____.

    c. True or false: _____ The first sentence of the story tells us a lot about the insult.

2. "And this was excellent for my purposes." (paragraph 4)
  a. "My" means (i) Poe's, (ii) Montressor's, (iii) Fortunato's.
  b. "This" means (i) Fortunato's knowledge of wines, (ii) Fortunato's pride in his knowledge of wines, (iii) both i and ii, (iv) Montressor's knowledge of wines.
  c. The "purposes" are (i) to enjoy Carnival, (ii) to taste some excellent old wine, (iii) to destroy Fortunato.

3. "'My dear Fortunato,' I said, 'how well you look!'" (paragraph 6)
  Montressor hates Fortunato, but here he speaks to him very warmly, like a good friend. Why does he do that? Can you find other sentences in Part I that express a similar "kindness" or "warmth" on the part of Montressor? (There are at least five of them.)

4. "Amontillado? A whole cask? Impossible! And in the middle of carnival!" (paragraph 7)
  On the basis of these words, and the words about Amontillado that follow them, how many of the statements below do you think are true about Amontillado? Explain.

  _____ **a.** Amontillado is easy to find at any time.

  _____ **b.** Amontillado is an expensive wine.

  _____ **c.** Anyone can tell the difference between Amontillado and ordinary wine.

  _____ **d.** Fortunato doesn't care for Amontillado.

5. "Since you are busy, I am going to find Luchresi. If anyone has the ability to judge, it is he." (paragraph 14)

From this quotation and the conversation which follows it, tell whether the following statements are true or false.

_____ **a.** Both Montressor and Fortunato know Luchresi.

_____ **b.** Montressor presents Luchresi as an expert on wines.

_____ **c.** Fortunato doesn't think Luchresi is a good judge of wines.

_____ **d.** Montressor really wants to find Luchresi to ask his opinion about the wine.

_____ **e.** Fortunato believes that Montressor might leave him to go find Luchresi.

C. Word Forms

Montressor feels he has been <u>insulted</u> by Fortunato. "I must have <u>revenge</u>," he says. Though he speaks no <u>threat</u>, he decides to <u>punish</u> Fortunato. We do not know how serious the <u>injury</u> to Fortunato will be. Will Montressor actually <u>destroy</u> the man he calls "my friend"?

The words underlined above are important to the idea of revenge in "The Cask of Amontillado." In this exercise, you are asked to select the appropriate word, and the correct forms of that word, for the blanks in each sentence below. The chart that follows will help you to select the correct word forms.

NOUN	VERB	ADJECTIVE/PARTICIPLE
insult	insult	insulting
insulter		insulted
revenge	revenge	revengeful
revenger		
punishment	punish	punishing
punisher		punished
injury	injure	injurious
		injured
destruction	destroy	destructful
destroyer		destroyed
		destroying
threat	threaten	threatening
		threatened

From the chart above, choose the word and its two forms that complete the blank spaces in each sentence below. (Each sentence should contain two forms of one word.)

1. According to Montressor, Fortunato has _____ him; yet when the two men meet on the street, Montressor's manner is not at all _____ . He acts in a very friendly, pleasant way.

2. Montressor speaks no _____ against Fortunato, because to _____ would be to reveal his intentions, and he wants to hide them.

3. We do not know what Fortunato has done to cause such _____ feelings in Montressor, but we know that Montressor feels he *must* have _____.

4. "The thousand _____ " that Montressor says he has suffered at the hands of Fortunato will be paid

back only when Montressor _____ Fortunato in
return.

5. Montressor smiles at Fortunato, and tells us that
inwardly this smile is at the thought of Fortunato's
_____. Does he intend to _____ Fortunato
completely? Does he mean to kill him?

6. Montressor says that the _____ must go free,
meaning that he must _____ without being seen.

PART II (PAGES 40–44)

**D. Close Reading: Understanding Irony of Expression and
Double Meanings**

In exercise F of "The Bride Comes to Yellow Sky," (page
33), you looked closely at some ironic moments in that
story. In this exercise, you are asked to look again at
some moments from "The Cask of Amontillado" when
Montressor *speaks* ironically—that is, when he says one
thing but means another. In talking to Fortunato,
Montressor often says something that has two meanings.
One meaning is for Fortunato, and the other, darkly
humorous, is for Montressor himself. Re-read the
following quotations from the story and answer the
questions about them.

1. "Enough!" he said. "The cough is a mere nothing I
shall not die of a cough."
"True, true," I replied. (paragraph 37)
When Montressor says "true, true," what does
Fortunato understand him to mean? What does he
really mean?

2. He said, "I drink to the members of your fine family
who are buried in these vaults."
"And I drink to your long life," I quietly replied.
(paragraphs 42 and 43)
The word "quietly" tells us that here again Montressor

is enjoying a private joke. What is it?

3. "You? Impossible! A Mason?"

"A real mason," I replied. (paragraph 52)

What does Fortunato mean by the word Mason? What does Montressor mean by the same word?

4. "Once more, I *beg* you to return with me. No? Then I must leave you. But first I should try to make you as comfortable as possible." (paragraph 60)

What, here, is Montressor's idea of "comfort"?

5. No answer still. I placed a torch through the last hole and let it fall inside. Only a small ringing of bells came in return. My heart grew sick; it was the dampness of the vault. (paragraph 76)

Perhaps Montressor himself is not aware of the double meaning of his words here. For us, is the "dampness of the vault" reason enough for Montressor's "sickness of heart"? What meaning do we see in his words here?

E. Language Activity: Speaking Ironically

Consider the following two short dialogues:

Student A: (Showing a photograph of the sun setting behind a mountain, with the sky full of reds, oranges, purples.) Well, do you like it? What do you think?

Student B: Very pretty!

Student A: (Showing a photograph of rotten old fruit, full of reds, oranges, purples.) Well, do you like it? What do you think?

Student B: Very pretty.

Of course, in the second dialogue, Student B is speaking ironically. He means the opposite of what he says. His tone of voice, and probably the look on his face, is very different from his first "Very pretty!"

With a partner (if possible), read the following short dialogues from "The Cask of Amontillado" out loud. Imagine what Montressor sounded like, and looked like, when he spoke the short, ironic sentences that end the dialogues.

1. Montressor: My dear Fortunato, I have received a cask of the real Amontillado wine.

    Fortunato: What, Montressor? Amontillado? The real thing?

    Montressor: I have my doubts.

    Fortunato: Amontillado!

    Montressor: I have my doubts.

    Fortunato: Amontillado!

    Montressor: And I must bury them.

2. Fortunato: Come, let us go.

    Montressor: Where?

    Fortunato: To your vaults.

    Montressor: My friend, no. I see that you are on your way to a party.

    Fortunato: I am going nowhere. Come.

    Montressor: My friend, no. I see you have a bad cold. My vaults are terribly damp. You will suffer.

3. Fortunato: Enough! The cough is a mere nothing ... I shall not die of a cough.

    Montressor: True, true.

4. Fortunato: I drink to the members of your fine family who are buried in these vaults.

    Montressor: And I drink to your long life.

5. Fortunato: You? Impossible! A Mason?

    Montressor: A real mason.

Try now yourself to write a short dialogue in which one of the two speakers speaks ironically. With a partner, read your dialogue to the class.

F. Vocabulary, Speaking, and Writing: Word Groups in "The Cask of Amontillado"

There are four major word groups in "The Cask of Amontillado"—that is, groups of words that we might associate with a particular idea or subject. These four groups are (1) words associated with Carnival, (2) words associated with Montressor's cellars, (3) words associated with plastering, (4) words associated with emotion in the story. Below are exercises for each of these four groups.

1. Words of the Carnival:

carnival	dusk	black silk
palazzo	tight pants	hat with bells
party	mask	crowded streets
brightly colored		

Using the above words, describe the meeting between Montressor and Fortunato on the street. Add words of your own; do not simply repeat the story.

2. Words of Montressor's cellars:

cellar	vault	dampness
staircase	torches	darkness
winding	burial	deep
bones	mold	underground
casks	bottles of wine	ceiling

Using the above words, describe the two men's journey down into the cellars and through the vaults. What did the vaults look like? What did they feel like?

3. Words of plastering:

plaster	mason	tool
trowel	building stone	to lay a row
wall	to plaster	

Using the above words, tell exactly how Montressor built the wall that closed Fortunato into the little room where he died.

4. Words that carry emotion:

insult	groan	violent
revenge	scream	furious
punish	laugh	horrify
pay back	beg	terrible

Using the above words, discuss both Montressor's and Fortunato's reactions to the events of the story. Use any form of the words given that fit your description.

G. Discussion: The Nature of Revenge

1. What was your reaction to "The Cask of Amontillado"? Were you satisfied, or horrified, that Montressor got his revenge on Fortunato? Did the story amuse you? frighten you? entertain you?

2. Do you think that Montressor is generally a dangerous man? Is he insane? What did you think of him while you were reading the story? What do you think of him now that you have finished the story?

3. Why do you think that the desire for revenge is such a powerful human feeling? Can you think of times in history when whole groups of people tried to revenge themselves for wrongs that had been done to them? What became of these attempts?

4. In the end, what does Montressor feel about the revenge he takes on Fortunato? (Re-read the final paragraph of the story.) Have you ever performed an act of revenge, even a small one? How did it make you feel?

Notes:

_____

_____

_____

_____

A JURY OF HER PEERS

Before You Read the Story ...

1. A Life

Read the paragraph about Susan Glaspell on page 55. What is the difference between the form of *Trifles* and the form of "A Jury of Her Peers"?

2. The Picture

Look at the picture on page 61. One woman is holding a *quilt block* in her hand. A *quilt* is a kind of bed cover. Small pieces (<u>blocks</u>) of cloth are sewed together to make a large cover. Then the quilt cover is sewed to heavier material to make the cover warm. There are two ways to fasten the top cover to the heavier material. One is to knot it—to tie it on with small knots. The other is to quilt it—to sew it on with small stitches.

3. Thinking About It ...

A *jury* is a group of people who study the facts in a law case and give a decision based on those facts. A *peer* is an equal, someone of the same value or quality or ability. In English and American law, each person accused of a crime has the right to argue his or her case before "a jury of his peers." If you needed to choose a jury of your peers to judge an action you had taken, which people would you choose? Why?

4. Scanning to Get an Impression

Sometimes we want to get a general idea, or impression, of a piece of writing before we read it carefully. To do this, we read quickly over the material, sometimes only a sentence or two from each paragraph. We don't try to understand details. We try only to get a general picture.

Quickly scan Part I (pages 56-57) of "A Jury of Her Peers," for no more than 30–40 seconds. Then try to answer the following questions.

a. Does the story take place in a warm climate, or a cold one?

b. Does the story take place in a city, or in the country?

c. Are the characters in the story men, or women, or both?

d. Does the story seem funny, or serious to you?

Now, read Part I more carefully, and answer each question above, using evidence from the story.

A JURY
OF
HER PEERS

adapted from the story by
SUSAN GLASPELL

Susan Glaspell was born in 1882, in Davenport, Iowa. She worked for a newspaper there until she earned enough to support herself by writing fiction. She wrote a lot—ten novels and more than 40 stories. But she is also well known for her plays. She and her husband founded the Provincetown Playhouse in Provincetown, Massachusetts (Cape Cod), in 1915. Her husband directed plays by young, unknown writers. Many of these writers later became famous. "A Jury of Her Peers" was first written as a play called Trifles—the word means "small things of little value." Glaspell often wrote about people trapped by the choices they make in life. Susan Glaspell died in 1948.

I

M artha Hale opened the storm door and felt the cutting North wind. She ran back inside for her big wool shawl. She was unhappy with what she saw there in her kitchen. Her bread was all ready for mixing, half the flour sifted and half unsifted. She hated to see things half done. But it was no ordinary thing that called her away. It was probably further from ordinary than anything that had ever happened in Dickson County.

2 She had been sifting flour when the sheriff drove up in the buggy to get Mr. Hale. Sheriff Peters had asked Mrs. Hale to come, too. His wife was nervous, he said with a grin. She wanted another woman to come along. So Martha Hale had dropped everything right where it was.

3 "Martha!" her husband's voice came, "Don't keep the folks waiting out here in the cold!"

4 She tied the wool shawl tighter and climbed into the buggy. Three men and a woman were waiting for her. Martha Hale had met Mrs. Peters, the sheriff's wife, at the county fair. Mrs. Peters didn't seem like a sheriff's wife. She was small and thin and ordinary. She didn't have a strong voice. But Mr. Peters certainly did look like a sheriff. He was a heavy man with a big voice, very friendly to folks who followed the law. But now, Mrs. Hale thought, he was going to the Wrights' house as a sheriff, not a friend.

5 The Wrights' house looked lonely this cold March morning. It had always been a lonely-looking house. It was down in a valley, and the poplar trees around it were lonely-looking trees. The men were talking about what had happened there: her husband, Sheriff Peters, and the county attorney, Mr. Henderson. She looked over at Mrs. Peters.

6 "I'm glad you came with me," Mrs. Peters said nervously.

7 When the buggy reached the doorstep, Martha Hale felt she could not go inside. She had often said to herself, "I must go over and see Minnie Foster." She still thought of her as Minnie Foster, though for twenty years she had been Mrs. Wright. But there was always something to do, and Minnie Foster would go from her mind. *Now* she could come.

8 The men went over to stand by the stove. The women stood together by the door. At first, they didn't even look around the kitchen.

9 "Now, Mr. Hale," the sheriff began. "Before we move things around, you tell Mr. Henderson what you saw when you came here yesterday morning."

II

10 Mrs. Hale felt nervous for her husband. Lewis Hale often lost his way in a story. She hoped he would tell it straight this time. Unnecessary things would just make it harder for Minnie Foster.

11 "Yes, Mr. Hale?" the county attorney said.

12 "I started to town with a load of potatoes," Mrs. Hale's husband began. "I came along this road, and I saw the house. I said to myself, 'I'm going to see John Wright about the telephone.' They will bring a telephone out here if I can get somebody else to help pay for it. I'd spoken to Wright before, but he said folks talked too much already. All *he* asked for was peace and quiet. I guess you know how much he talked himself! But I thought I would ask him in front of his wife. All the women like the telephone. In this lonely road it would be a good thing. Not that he cared much about what his wife wanted ..."

13 Now there he was!—saying things he didn't need to say. Mrs. Hale tried to catch her husband's eye, but luckily the attorney interrupted him with:

14 "Just tell what happened when you got there, Mr. Hale."

15 Mr. Hale began again, more carefully. "I knocked at the door. But it was all quiet inside. I knew they must be up—it was past eight o'clock. I knocked again, louder, and I thought I heard someone say, 'Come in.' I opened the door—this door"—Mr. Hale pointed toward the door where the two women stood. "And there, in that rocking-chair"—he pointed to it—"sat Mrs. Wright."

16 "How did she—look?" the county attorney asked.

17 "Well," said Hale, "she looked—strange."

18 "How do you mean—strange?"

19 The attorney took out a notebook and pencil. Mrs. Hale did not like that pencil. She kept her eye on her husband, as if to tell him, "No unnecessary things. They'll just go into that notebook and make trouble." Hale spoke carefully, as if the pencil made him think more slowly.

20 "Well, she didn't seem to know what she was going to do next. I said, 'How do, Mrs. Wright. It's cold isn't it?' And she said, 'Is it?,' and sat there pleating her apron.

21 "Well, I was surprised. She didn't ask me to come in and sit down, but just sat there, not even looking at me. And so I said, 'I want to see John.'

22 "And then she—laughed. I guess you'd call it a laugh.

23 "I said, a little sharp, 'Can I see John?'

24 "'No,' she said, kind of dull. "Isn't he home?' said I. 'Yes,' says she, 'he's home.' 'Then why can't I see him?' I asked her. Now I was angry. 'Because he's dead,' says she— all quiet and dull. She pleated her apron some more.

25 "'Why, where is he?' I said, not knowing *what* to say.

26 "She just pointed upstairs—like this," said Hale, pointing. "Then I said, 'Why, what did he die of?'

27 "'He died of a rope around his neck,' says she, and just went on pleating her apron."

28 Nobody spoke. Everyone looked at the rocking-chair as if they saw the woman who had sat there yesterday.

29 "And what did you do then?" the attorney at last interrupted the silence.

30 "I went upstairs." Hale's voice fell. "There he was— lying on the—He was dead, all right. I thought I'd better

not touch anything. So I went downstairs.

31 "'Who did this, Mrs. Wright?'" I said, sharp, and she stops pleating her apron. 'I don't know,' she says. 'You don't know?' said I. 'Weren't you sleeping in the same bed with him? Somebody tied a rope around his neck and killed him, and you didn't wake up?'

32 "'I didn't wake up,' she says after me.

33 "I may have looked as if I didn't see how that could be. After a minute she said, 'I sleep sound.'"

34 "I thought maybe she ought to tell her story first to the sheriff. So I went as fast as I could to the nearest telephone—over at the Rivers' place on High Road. Then I came back here to wait for Sheriff Peters.

35 "I thought I should talk to her. So I said I had stopped by to see if John wanted to put in a telephone. At that, she started to laugh, and then she stopped and looked frightened ...."

36 The attorney spoke to the sheriff. "I guess we'll go upstairs first—then out to the barn and around there. You made sure yesterday that there's nothing important here in the kitchen?"

37 "Nothing here but kitchen things," said the sheriff with a laugh."

38 The attorney was searching in the cupboard. After a minute he pulled out his hand, all sticky.

39 "Here's a nice mess," he said angrily.

40 "Oh—her fruit," Mrs. Peters said. She looked at Mrs. Hale. "She was worried bout her fruit when it turned cold last night. She said the stove might go out, and the jars might break."

41 Mrs. Peters' husband began to laugh. "Well, how about that for a woman! Held for murder, and worrying about her jars of fruit!"

42 The attorney answered, "I guess before we finish with her, she may have something more important to worry about."

43 "Oh, well," Mr. Hale said, "women are used to worrying about nothing."

44 "And yet," said the attorney, "what would we do

without the ladies?" He smiled at the women, but they did not speak, did not smile back.

45 The lawyer washed his hands and dried them on the dishtowel.

46 "Dirty towels!" he said. "Not much of a housekeeper, eh, ladies?" He kicked some messy pans under the sink.

47 "There's a lot of work to do around a farm," Mrs. Hale said sharply. "and men's hands aren't always as clean as they might be."

48 "Ah! You feel a duty to your sex, I see!" He laughed. "But you and Mrs. Wright were neighbors. I guess you were friends, too."

49 "I've not seen much of her these years."

50 "And why was that? You didn't like her?"

51 "I liked her well enough. Farmers' wives have their hands full, Mr. Henderson. And then—it never seemed like a very happy place ..."

52 "You mean the Wrights didn't get on very well together?"

53 "No. I don't mean anything. But I don't think a place would be happier if John Wright was in it."

54 "I'd like to talk to you more about that, Mrs. Hale. But first we'll look upstairs."

55 The sheriff said to the attorney, "I suppose anything Mrs. Peters does will be all right? She came to take Mrs. Wright some clothes—and a few little things."

56 "Of course," said the attorney. "Mrs. Peters is one of us. Maybe you women may come on a clue to the motive— and that's the thing we need."

57 Mr. Hale smiled, ready to make a joke. "Yes, but would the women know a clue if they did come upon it?"

III

58 The women stood silent while the men went upstairs. Then Mrs. Hale began to clean the messy pans under the sink.

59 "I would hate to have men coming into my kitchen, looking around and talking about my housework."

60 "Of course, it's their duty," Mrs. Peters said. But Mrs. Hale was looking around the kitchen herself. She saw a box of sugar. Next to it was a paper bag—half full.

61 "She was putting this in there," she said to herself. Work begun and not finished? She saw the table—a dishtowel lay on it. One-half of the table was clean. What had interrupted Minnie Foster?

62 "I must get her things from the cupboard," Mrs. Peters said.

63 Together they found the few clothes Mrs. Wright had asked for. Mrs. Hale picked up an old black skirt.

64 "My, John Wright hated to spend money!" she said. "She used to wear pretty clothes and sing in the church, when she was Minnie Foster ..." Martha Hale looked at Mrs. Peters and thought: she doesn't care that Minnie Foster had pretty clothes when she was a girl. But then she looked at Mrs. Peters again, and she wasn't sure. In fact, she had never been sure of Mrs. Peters. She seemed so nervous, but her eyes looked as if they could see a long way into things.

65 "Is this all you want to take to the jail?" Martha Hale asked.

66 "No, she wanted an apron and her woolen shawl." Mrs. Peters took them from the cupboard.

67 "Mrs. Peters!" cried Mrs. Hale suddenly. "Do you think she did it?"

68 Mrs. Peters looked frightened. "Oh, I don't know," she said.

69 "Well, I don't think she did," Mrs. Hale said. "Asking for her apron and her shawl. Worrying about her fruit."

70 "Mr. Peters says it looks bad for her," Mrs. Peters answered. "Saying she didn't wake up when someone tied that rope around his neck. Mr. Henderson said that what this case needs is a motive. Something to show anger—or sudden feeling."

71 "Well, I think it's kind of low to lock her up in jail, and then come out here to look for clues in her own

house," said Martha Hale.

72 "But, Mrs. Hale, " said the sheriff's wife, "The law is the law."

73 Mrs. Hale turned to re-light the stove. "How would you like to cook on this broken thing year after year—?"

74 Mrs. Peters looked from the broken stove to the bucket of water on the sink. Water had to be carried in from outside. "I know. A person gets so *down*—and loses heart."

75 And again Mrs. Peters' eyes had that look of seeing into things, of seeing through things.

76 "Oh, look, Mrs. Hale. She was sewing a quilt." Mrs. Peters picked up a sewing basket full of quilt blocks.

77 The women were studying the quilt as the men came downstairs. Just as the door opened, Mrs. Hale was saying, "Do you think she was going to quilt it, or just knot it?"

78 "Quilt it or knot it!" laughed the sheriff. "They're worrying about a quilt!" The men went out to look in the barn.

79 Then Mrs. Peters said in a strange voice, "Why, look at this one." She held up a quilt block. "The sewing. All the rest were sewed so nice. But this one is so *messy*—"

80 Mrs. Hale took the quilt block. She pulled out the sewing and started to replace bad sewing with good.

81 "Oh, I don't think we ought to touch anything ..." Mrs. Peters said helplessly.

82 "I'll just finish this end," said Mrs. Hale, quietly.

83 "Mrs. Hale?"

84 "Yes, Mrs. Peters?"

85 "What do you think she was so *nervous* about?"

86 "Oh, *I* don't know. I don't know that she was— nervous. Sometimes I sew badly when I'm tired."

87 She looked quickly at Mrs. Peters, but Mrs. Peters was looking far away. Later she said in an ordinary voice, "Here's a bird cage. Did she have a bird, Mrs. Hale? It seems kind of funny to think of a bird here. I wonder what happened to it."

88 "Oh, probably the cat got it."

89 "But look, the door has been broken. It looks as if someone was rough with it."

90 Their eyes met, worrying and wondering.

91 "I'm glad you came with me, Mrs. Hale. It would be lonely for me—sitting here alone."

92 "I *wish* I had come over here sometimes when she was here," answered Mrs. Hale. I stayed away because it wasn't a happy place. Did you know John Wright, Mrs. Peters?"

93 "Not really. They say he was a good man."

94 "Well—good," Mrs. Hale said. "He didn't drink, and paid his bills. But he was a hard man. His voice was like the north wind that cuts to the bone. You didn't know—her, did you, Mrs. Peters?"

95 "Not until they brought her to the jail yesterday,"

96 "She was—she was like a little bird herself ... Why don't you take the quilt blocks in to her? It might take up her mind."

97 "That's a nice idea, Mrs. Hale," agreed the sheriff's wife. She took more quilt blocks and a small box out of the sewing basket.

98 "What a pretty box," Mrs. Hale said. "That must be something she had from a long time ago, when she was a girl." Mrs. Hale opened the box. Quickly her hand went to her nose.

99 Mrs. Peters bent closer. "It's the bird," she said softly. "Someone broke its neck."

100 Just then the men came in the door. Mrs. Hale slipped the box under the quilt blocks.

101 "Well, ladies," said the county attorney, "have you decided if she was going to quilt it or knot it?" He smiled at them.

102 "We think," began the sheriff's wife nervously, "that she was going to—knot it."

103 "That's interesting, I'm sure," he said, not listening. "Well, there's no sign that someone came in from the outside. And it was their own rope. Now let's go upstairs again ..." The men left the kitchen again.

104 "She was going to bury the bird in that pretty

box," said Mrs. Hale.

105 "When I was a girl," said Mrs. Peters softly, "my kitten—there was a boy who murdered it, in front of my eyes. If they hadn't held me back, I would have—hurt him."

106 They sat without speaking or moving.

107 "Wright wouldn't like the bird. A thing that sang. *She* used to sing. He killed that, too," Mrs. Hale said slowly.

108 "Of course, we don't *know* who killed the bird," said Mrs. Peters.

109 "I knew John Wright," Mrs. Hale answered. "There had been years and years of—nothing. Then she had a bird to sing to her. It would be so—silent—when it stopped."

110 "I know what silence is," Mrs. Peters said in a strange voice. "When my first baby died, after two years ..."

111 "Oh, I *wish* I'd come over here sometimes. *That* was a crime!" Mrs. Hale cried.

112 But the men were coming back. "No, Peters, it's all clear. Except the reason for doing it. If there was some real *clue* .... Something to show the jury .... You go back to town, sheriff. I'll stay and look around some more."

113 Mrs. Hale looked at Mrs. Peters. Mrs. Peters was looking at her.

114 "Do you want to see what Mrs. Peters is bringing to the jail?" the sheriff asked the attorney.

115 "Oh, I guess the ladies haven't picked up anything very dangerous," he answered. "After all, a sheriff's wife is married to the law. Did you ever think of your duty that way, Mrs. Peters?"

116 "Not—just that way," said Mrs. Peters quietly.

117 The men went out to get the buggy, and the women were alone for one last moment.

118 Mrs. Hale pointed to the sewing-basket. In it was the thing that would keep another woman in jail.

119 For a moment Mrs. Peters did not move. Then she ran to get the box. She tried to put it in her handbag, but it was too big.

120 There was the sound of the door opening. Martha Hale took the box and put it quickly in her pocket.

121 "Well, Peters," said the county attorney jokingly,

"at least we found out that she was not going to quilt it. She was going to—what do you call it, ladies?"

122 Mrs. Hale put her hand against her pocket. "We call it—knot it, Mr. Henderson."

A JURY OF HER PEERS
EXERCISES

A. Understanding the Plot of the Story

Answer the following questions with complete sentences.

1. What was Martha Hale doing when the sheriff arrived? Why did the sheriff want her to come with the others?

2. What did Lewis Hale find when he stopped at the Wright's house?

3. What do the men say about Mrs. Wright's housekeeping?

4. What do the sheriff and the attorney need to find for the jury?

5. What do the women notice about one of the quilt blocks? What does Martha do with it?

6. What was in the small box the women found in the sewing basket?

7. What does Martha do with the box? Why?

PART I (PAGES 56–57)

B. Close Reading: Who's Who

The first section of "A Jury of Her Peers" introduces us to a number of people. To know "who's who," we have to read closely. Identify the names below with the descriptions of people listed below the names. Next to each description, write the name of the person who fits the description. Some names are used more than once.

Mrs. Hale	Mr. Hale	Mr. Peters
Mr. Henderson	Mrs. Peters	
Mr. and Mrs. Wright	Minnie Foster	

1. _____ He is the county attorney.

2. _____ He saw something interesting at the Wrights' house yesterday morning.

3. _____ She is small and thin and has a weak voice.

4. _____ She was making bread when the others came to her house.

5. _____ She became Mrs. Wright.

6. _____ All the others were going to their house.

7. _____ He is the county sheriff, and a big man.

8. _____ He asked his wife not to keep everybody waiting in the buggy, in the cold.

9. _____ She was glad that Martha had come on this trip.

10. _____ She hated to leave things half done, but this situation was very unusual.

PART II (PAGES 57–60)

C. Word Forms

For each group of sentences below, give the correct form of the word given.

1. nervous, nervousness, nervously

  a. Mrs. Hale felt _____ for her husband.

  b. Mrs. Wright tried to hide her _____ by laughing.

  c. Mrs. Peters looked away _____ from Mrs. Hale.

2. unnecessary, unnecessarily

  a. Mrs. Peters worried _____ about being alone at the Wright's house.

b. Mrs. Hale hoped that her husband would leave out

_____ details from his story.

3. peace, peaceful, peacefully

a. Although Mr. Wright liked peace and quiet, he was

not a _____ man.

b. After the sheriff arrested her, Mrs. Wright

went _____ to jail.

c. Mrs. Hale's _____ of mind was broken by news

of Wright's murder.

4. duty, dutiful, dutifully

a. When the attorney said that Mrs. Peters was "one of

us," he wanted to remind her that she had

a _____ to follow the law.

b. Is Mrs. Hale a less _____ woman than Mrs.

Peters?

c. Every summer Mrs. Wright _____ makes jars of

fruit for winter use.

5. trouble, troubled, troublesome

a. Mr. Hale thought Mrs. Wright acted _____

about something.

b. The sheriff was sure they wouldn't find any _____

clues in the kitchen.

c. Mrs. Hale hoped her husband wouldn't bring any

more _____ to Mrs. Wright.

6. mess, messy, messily

a. Mrs. Wright tells the attorney that there are good

reasons for _____ housekeeping.

b. The broken fruit jars made a _____ in the cupboard.

c. Mrs. Wright's pots and pans were pushed _____ under the sink.

D. Vocabulary

Match the words in column A with the correct definitions in column B by writing the appropriate number in the blanks. Then write your own sentence with each of the five words.

A	B
1. county	___ **a.** what causes a person to do something
2. attorney	___ **b.** an unlawful killing
3. clue	___ **c.** an area consisting of two or more towns
4. murder	___ **d.** something that helps solve a problem
5. motive	___ **e.** an officer of a court of law

1. county

_____

_____

2. attorney

_____

_____

3. murder

_____

_____

4. clue

_____

_____

5. motive

_____

_____

E. Close Reading: Implied Meaning in Dialogue

Often, a writer will use dialogue that suggests, rather than states directly, how one character feels about another. A better word for this kind of suggestion is *implication,* or implied meaning. The sentences below from part II are good examples of implied meaning. The questions which follow ask you to tell what the words of each speaker *imply.* Paragraph numbers are given so that you can find the dialogue in the story.

1. "Nothing here but kitchen things," said the sheriff with a laugh. (paragraph 37)
What is implied here by the sheriff's laugh? What does he think about the value of "kitchen things"?

_____

_____

2. "Well, how about that for a woman! Held for murder, and worrying about her fruit!" (paragraph 41)
What does the sheriff imply about the woman's interest in her fruit? What does he imply about women generally?

_____

_____

3. "Oh, well," Mr. Hale said, "women are used to worrying about nothing." (paragraph 43)
In saying that "women are used to worrying about

nothing," what does Mr. Hale imply about the seriousness of women's concerns generally?

_____

_____

4. "And yet," said the attorney, "what would we do without the ladies?" (paragraph 44)
The attorney seems to be saying that "the ladies" are valuable to "us." But he implies something different. What is it?
Read the rest of the paragraph. What do Mrs. Hale and Mrs. Peters imply by their reaction to him?

_____

_____

5. "There's a lot of work to do around a farm," Mrs. Hale said sharply. "And men's hands aren't always as clean as they might be." (paragraph 47)
What does Mrs. Hale imply here about the habits of men on a farm?

_____

_____

PART III (PAGES 60–66)

F. Language Activities: The Clues and a Trial

1. What are the clues that lead Mrs. Hale and Mrs. Peters to an understanding of what Mrs. Wright did, and why she did it?
With a partner (if possible), re-read Part III and find the specific clues that the two women discovered. There are at least four important ones, as well as some smaller ones. Be prepared to describe the clues and tell why they are important.

2. Is Minnie Foster guilty, or innocent, of the crime with which she will be charged? Did Minnie Foster murder her husband?

Choose among the class a *judge* and two attorneys—one a *prosecuting* attorney, the other a *defense* attorney. Choose several class members to serve on the jury. Let others be called as *witnesses*: Mr. and Mrs. Hale, Sheriff and Mrs. Peters, and other friends and neighbors. Hold the trial. Let the jury consider the *evidence* and give the *verdict*, and let the judge decide the *sentence*, if she is found guilty. The words underlined in this paragraph will help you. Make sure you understand their meaning before you start.

G. Writing: A Dialogue

"A Jury of Her Peers" is told almost completely in dialogue—there is very little description. Write a page of dialogue: a conversation among Mrs. Hale, Mrs. Peters, and Mrs. Wright. Mrs. Hale and Mrs. Peters visit Mrs. Wright in the county jail. They bring her the things she has asked for. What do they talk about? What does she answer? Try to have the women speak and act as they do in the story.

H. Discussion: Attitudes and Responsibilities

1. An important theme of "A Jury of Her Peers" concerns the activities and duties of men and women at the time that the story was written. Discuss what men expected from women, and women from men. Support your discussion with examples from the story. Have these attitudes changed, today? Why or why not?

2. What do Mrs. Hale and Mrs. Peters do with the clues that they find? Aren't these clues evidence of murder? Is it wrong of them not to give the clues to the sheriff? Why, or why not?

Notes:

_____

_____

_____

PASTE

Before You Read the Story ...

1. *A Life*

Read the paragraph about Henry James on page 75. List at least three reasons why a person might want to change his or her citizenship. Does any of them seem to fit Henry James? Why do you think he became a British citizen?

2. *The Pictures*

Look at the pictures on pages 77 and 82. One object, and one person, are common to both pictures. What are they?

3. *Thinking About It ...*

The word *paste* in the title of the story has a special meaning. It does not mean the soft mixture used to glue paper, or to brush your teeth. "Paste," here, means a mixture used to make artificial (not real; false) jewelry. The story is about jewels, real or false, and qualities in people's characters that might also be called real or false. What are some of the qualities that people often show to the outside world that are not real, but false?

4. *Scanning Different Sources of Information*

For this exercise you will need to use the paragraphs about Stephen Crane (page 17), Edgar Allen Poe (page 37), Susan Glaspell (page 55), and Henry James (page 75).

Sometimes we need to find small, specific pieces of information from more than one source of information. In order to find the information asked for in the questions below, let your eyes move quickly over the four paragraphs mentioned above until you find the name, date, or words underlined in the question. Then read more quickly until you can answer the question. Try to answer all the questions in less than ten minutes.

a. How old was Poe when he died?

b. What is the novel, The Red Badge of Courage, about?

c. Which writer had a brother who was a famous philosopher?

d. Which writer lived for a time on Cape Cod in Massachusetts?

e. Which writer received an education in law?

f. Which writers were *not* born in New York, Massachusetts, or New Jersey?

g. Which writer was an editor for literary magazines?

h. Which writer lived the longest?

PASTE

adapted from the story by
HENRY JAMES

Henry James was born in 1843 in Washington Place, New York. His father was a well-known religious thinker; his older brother, William James, became a famous philosopher. James was educated in New York and Europe and attended Harvard Law School. His years of school in London, Paris, and Geneva gave him a love for Europe. He traveled often to Europe, and after 1876 made his home in London. James wrote widely. In addition to plays, criticism, and short stories, he wrote about twenty novels. The Europeans, Washington Square, The Portrait of a Lady, and The Bostonians are among the best known. Much of James's work deals with the contrast in values and behavior of Americans and Europeans. He became a British citizen shortly before his death in 1916.

I

"I've found a lot more of her things," Charlotte's cousin said to her after his stepmother's funeral. "They're up in her room—but they're things I wish *you'd* look at."

2 Charlotte and her cousin, Arthur Prime, were in his father's, the minister's, garden, waiting for lunch. It seemed to Charlotte that Arthur's face showed the wish to express some kind of feeling. It was not surprising that Arthur should feel something. His stepmother had recently died, only three weeks after his father's death.

3 Charlotte had no money of her own and lived with a wealthy family as governess for their children. She had asked for leave to attend the funeral. During her stay Charlotte had noticed that her cousin seemed somehow to grieve without sorrow, to suffer without pain. It was Arthur's habit to drop a comment and leave her to pick it up without help. What "things" did he mean now? However, since she hoped for a remembrance of her step-aunt, she went to look at these "things" he had spoken of.

4 As she entered the darkened room, Charlotte's eyes were struck by the bright jewels which glowed on the table. Even before touching them, she guessed they were things of the theater. They were much too fine to have been things of the minister's wife. Her step-aunt had had no jewelry to speak of, and these were crowns and necklaces, diamonds and gold. After her first shock, Charlotte picked them up. They seemed like proof of the far-off, faded story of her step-aunt's life. Her uncle, a country minister, had lost his first wife. With a small son, Arthur, and a large admiration for the theater, he had developed an even

larger admiration for an unknown actress. He had offered his hand in marriage. Still more surprisingly, the actress had accepted. Charlotte had suspected for years that her step-aunt's acting could not have brought her either fame or fortune.

5 "You see what it is—old stuff of the time she never liked to mention."

6 Charlotte jumped a little. Arthur must have followed her upstairs. He was watching her slightly nervous recognition of the jewelry.

7 "I thought so myself," she replied. Then, to show intelligence without sounding silly, she said, "How odd they look!"

8 "They look awful," said Arthur Prime. "Cheap glass diamonds as big as potatoes. Actors have better taste now."

9 "Oh," said Charlotte, wanting to sound as knowledgeable as he, "now actresses have real diamonds."

10 "Some of them do."

11 "Oh, I mean even the bad ones—the nobodies, too."

12 Arthur replied coldly, "Some of the nobodies have the biggest jewels. But Mama wasn't *that* sort of actress."

13 "A nobody?" Charlotte asked.

14 "She wasn't a nobody that someone would give—well, not a nobody with diamonds. This stuff is worthless."

15 There was something about the old theater pieces that attracted Charlotte. She continued to turn them over in her hands.

16 Arthur paused, then he asked: "Do you care for them? I mean, as a remembrance?"

17 "Of you?" Charlotte said quickly.

18 "Of me? What do I have to do with it? Of your poor, dead aunt, who was so kind to you," he said virtuously.

19 "Well, I would rather have them than nothing."

20 "Then please take them." His face expressed more hope than generosity.

21 "Thank you." Charlotte lifted two or three pieces up and then set them down again. They were light, but so large and false that they made an awkward gift.

22 "Did you know she had kept them?"

23 "I don't believe she knew they were there, and I'm sure my father didn't. Her connection with the theater was over. These things were just put in a corner and forgotten."

24 Charlotte wondered, "What corner had she found to put them in?"

25 "She hadn't *found* it, she'd lost it," Arthur insisted. "The whole thing had passed from her mind after she put the stuff into a box in the schoolroom cupboard. The box had been stuck there for years."

26 "Are you sure they're not worth anything?" Charlotte asked dreamily.

27 But Arthur Prime had already asked himself this question and found the answer.

28 "If they had been worth anything, she would have sold them long ago. Unfortunately, my father and she were never wealthy enough to keep things of value locked up."

29 He looked at Charlotte for agreement and added, like one who is unfamiliar with generosity, "And if they're worth anything at all—why, you're all the more welcome to them."

30 Charlotte picked up a small silk bag. As she opened it she answered him, "I shall like them. They're all I have."

31 "All you have—?"

32 "That belonged to her."

33 He looked around the poor room as if to question her greed. "Well, what else do you want?"

34 "Nothing. Thank you very much." As she said this she looked into the small silk bag. It held a necklace of large pearls.

35 "Perhaps this *is* worth something. Feel it." She passed him the necklace.

36 He weighed it in his hands without interest. "Worthless, I'm sure—it's paste."

37 "But *is* it paste?"

38 He spoke impatiently. "Pearls nearly as large as nuts?"

39 "But they're heavy," Charlotte insisted.

40 "No heavier than anything else," he said, as if

amused at her simplicity.

41 Charlotte studied them a little, feeling them, turning them around.

42 "Couldn't they possibly be real?"

43 "Of that size? Put away with that stuff?"

44 "Well, I admit it's not likely," Charlotte said. "And pearls are so easily imitated."

45 "Pearls are *not* easily imitated, to anyone who knows about them. These have no shine. Anyway, how would she have got them?"

46 "Couldn't they have been a present?" Charlotte asked.

47 Arthur looked at her as if she had said something improper. "You mean because actresses are approached by men who—" He stopped suddenly. "No, they couldn't have been a present," he said sharply, and left the room.

48 Later, in the evening, they met to discuss Charlotte's departure the next day. At the end of the conversation, Arthur said.

49 "I really can't let you think that my stepmother was at *any* time of her life a woman who could—"

50 "Accept expensive presents from admirers?" Charlotte added. Somehow Arthur always made her speak more directly than she meant to. But he only answered, seriously,

51 "Exactly."

52 "I didn't think of that, when I spoke this morning", said Charlotte apologetically, "but I see what you mean."

53 "I mean that her virtue was above question," said Arthur Prime.

54 "A hundred times yes."

55 "Therefore she could never have afforded such pearls on her small salary."

56 "Of *course* she couldn't," Charlotte answered comfortingly. "Anyway," she continued, "I noticed that the clasp that holds the pearls together isn't even gold. I suppose it wouldn't be, with false pearls."

57 "The whole thing is cheap paste," Arthur announced, as if to end their discussion. "If the pearls were

real, and she had hidden them all these years—"

58 "Yes?" asked Charlotte curiously.

59 "Well, I wouldn't know *what* to think!"

60 "Oh, I see," said Charlotte, and their conversation ended.

II

61 When she was back at work again, the false jewels seemed silly to Charlotte. She wasn't sure why she had taken them. She put them away under a pile of clothing, and there they might have stayed, except for the arrival of Mrs. Guy.

62 Mrs. Guy was a strange little woman with red hair and black dresses. She had the face of a baby, but took command like a general. She was a friend of the family Charlotte worked for. She had come to organize a week of parties to celebrate the 21st birthday of the family's oldest son. She happily accepted Charlotte's help with the entertainments.

63 "Tomorrow and Thursday are all right, but we need to plan something for Friday evening," she announced to Charlotte.

64 "What would you like to do?"

65 "Well, plays are my strong point, you know," said Mrs. Guy.

66 They discussed plays and looked at the hats and dresses they might wear.

67 "But we need something to brighten these up," Mrs. Guy decided. "These things are too dull. Haven't you got anything else?"

68 "Well, I do have a few things ..." Charlotte admitted slowly. She went to find the jewels for Mrs. Guy. "Perhaps they're too bright, they're just glass and paste."

69 "Larger than life!" Mrs. Guy was excited. "They are just what we need. They'll give me great ideas!"

70 The next morning she came to find Charlotte in the schoolroom.

71 "I don't understand where you got these pieces," she said to Charlotte.

72 "They belonged to my aunt, who died a few months ago. She was an actress for several years. They were part of her equipment."

73 "She left them to you?"

74 "No; my cousin, her stepson, who naturally has no use for them, gave them to me as a remembrance of her. She was a dear, kind person, always so nice to me, and I was very fond of her."

75 Mrs. Guy listened with interest. "But it must be your *cousin* who is a 'dear, kind person.' Is *he* also 'always so nice' to you?"

76 "What do you mean?" asked Charlotte.

77 "Can't you guess?"

78 A strange feeling came over Charlotte. "The pearls—" she started to say.

79 "Doesn't your cousin know either?"

80 Charlotte felt herself turning pink. "They're *not* paste?"

81 "Haven't you looked at them?" Mrs. Guy continued.

82 Charlotte felt ashamed. Not to have known that the pearls were real!

83 "Come to my room when you finish teaching," Mrs. Guy ordered, "You'll see!"

84 Later, in Mrs. Guy's room, Charlotte stared at the pearls around Mrs. Guy's neck. Surely they were the only mysterious thing her step-aunt had owned.

85 "What in the world have you done to them?"

86 "I only handled them, understood them, admired them and put them on," Mrs. Guy answered proudly. "That's what pearls need. They need to be worn—it wakes them up. They're alive, you see. How have these been treated? They must have been buried, ignored. They were half dead. Don't you *know* about pearls?"

87 "How could I have known?" said penniless Charlotte. "Do you?"

88 "I know everything about pearls. These were simply asleep. From the moment I touched them you could see they were real."

89 "I couldn't see," admitted Charlotte, "although I

did wonder about them. Then their value—"

90 "Oh, their value is excellent!"

91 Charlotte felt dizzy. "But my cousin didn't know. He thinks they're worthless."

92 "Because the rest of the jewels are false? Then your cousin is a fool. But, anyway, he gave them to you."

93 "But if he gave them to me because he thought they were worthless—"

94 "You think you must give them back? I don't agree. If he was such a fool that he didn't recognize their value, it's his fault."

95 Charlotte looked at the pearls. They *were* beautiful. At the moment, however, they seemed to belong more to Mrs. Guy than to Charlotte *or* her cousin. She said finally:

96 "Yes, he insisted that the pearls were paste, even after I clearly said they looked different from the other things."

97 "Well, then, you see!" said Mrs. Guy. Her voice expressed more than victory over Arthur Prime—she sounded relieved.

98 But Charlotte was still not sure. "You see, he thought they couldn't be different because they shouldn't be."

99 "Shouldn't be? I don't understand."

100 "Well, how would she have got them?" Charlotte asked directly.

101 "Do you mean she might have stolen them?"

102 "No, but she had been an actress."

103 "Well, then!" cried Mrs. Guy. "That's exactly how she got them."

104 "Yes, but she wasn't famous or rich."

105 "Was she ugly?" Mrs. Guy inquired.

106 "No. She must have looked rather nice when she was young."

107 "Well, then!" cried Mrs. Guy again, as if she had proved her point.

108 "You mean the pearls were a present? That's just the idea my cousin dislikes—that she had such a generous admirer."

109 "And that she wouldn't have taken the pearls for nothing? I should think not! Let's hope she gave him *something* in return. Let's hope she was kind to him."

110 "Well," Charlotte continued, "I suppose she must have been 'kind' as you call it. That's why none of us knew she had something so valuable. That's why she had to hide them."

111 "You're suggesting that she was ashamed of them?"

112 "Well, she had married a minister."

113 "But he married *her*. What did he think of her past life?"

114 "Well, that she was not the sort of woman who encouraged such gifts."

115 "Ah! my dear! What woman is *not!*" said Mrs. Guy with a smile.

116 "And I don't want to give away her secret," continued Charlotte. "I liked her very much."

117 "Then don't!" decided Mrs. Guy. "Keep them."

118 "It's so difficult!" sighed Charlotte. "I must think. I'll tell you tonight, after I decide what to do."

119 "But may I wear them—this evening at dinner?" Mrs. Guy's hands held the pearls lovingly.

120 It was probably Mrs. Guy's possessiveness that decided Charlotte; but for the moment she only said, "As you like," before she closed the door.

121 It was almost eleven o'clock before Charlotte had a chance to meet with Mrs. Guy again. Mrs. Guy had worn the pearls to dinner, and announced that they had been "A great success, my dear, a sensation!"

122 "They *are* beautiful," Charlotte agreed, "but I can't be silent."

123 "Then you plan to return them?"

124 "If I don't, I'll be a thief."

125 "If you do, you're a fool!" said Mrs. Guy angrily.

126 "Well, of the two ..." Charlotte answered faintly.

127 Mrs. Guy interrupted her. "You won't tell him I told you that they're real, will you?"

128 "No, certainly not."

129 "Then, perhaps he won't believe you, and he will give them back to us!" And feeling much better, Mrs. Guy went to bed.

130 But Charlotte didn't like to return the pearls to Arthur Prime by mail, and was too busy to go to town herself. On the last day of Mrs. Guy's visit, she came to Charlotte.

131 "Come now, how much will you sell them for?"

132 "The pearls? Oh, you'll have to bargain with my cousin."

133 "Where does he live?"

134 Charlotte gave her the address.

135 "But how can I talk with him if you don't do anything about returning them?" Mrs. Guy complained.

136 "Oh, I *will.* I'm only waiting until the family goes to town. Do you want the pearls so much?"

137 "I'm dying for them. There's a special mystery about them. They have a white glow." Mrs. Guy paused. "My dear," she whispered, "they're things of love!"

138 "Oh, dear!" cried Charlotte.

139 "They're things of passion!"

140 "Oh, heavens!"

III

141 Mrs. Guy left, but Charlotte couldn't forget her words. She felt she had a new view of her dear, dead aunt. Had her step-aunt suffered over the pearls, hidden away with the false jewels? Charlotte began wearing the pearls in private; she came to feel a strange attachment to them. But still she was poor, and she dreamed that Arthur Prime might show an uncharacteristic generosity and say to her:

142 "Oh, keep the pearls! Of course, I couldn't afford to give them to you if I had known their value. But since you *have* got them, and found out the truth yourself, I really can't take them away from you."

143 In fact, his reaction was quite different when she finally went to town to tell him her story.

144 "I don't believe in them," he said. He was angry

and pale.

145 "That's exactly what I wanted to hear," Charlotte replied.

146 "It's a most unpleasant, improper suggestion," he added. "To think that she ..."

147 "If you're afraid to believe they're real, it's not my fault."

148 Arthur said nothing for a while. Then he picked them up. "They're what I said originally. They're only paste."

149 "Then may I keep them?"

150 "No. I want a better opinion."

151 "Better than your opinion."

152 "No. Better than *yours*." Arthur took the pearls and locked them in a drawer.

153 "You say I'm afraid," he added. "But I won't be afraid to take them to a jeweler to ask for an opinion."

154 "And if he says they're real?"

155 "He won't say so. He couldn't," Arthur insisted.

156 Two weeks later Charlotte received a letter about the pearls from Arthur. Still later Mrs. Guy was invited to dinner by Charlotte's employer. She was wearing a beautiful string of pearls.

157 "Do you see?" She came over to greet Charlotte, pointing at her necklace.

158 Charlotte wore a sickly smile. "They're almost as nice as Arthur's," she said.

159 "Almost? Where are your eyes, my dear? They *are* Arthur's. I tracked them to the jeweler's window where he sold them."

160 "*Sold* them?" Charlotte was horrified. "He wrote me that I had insulted his stepmother and that the jeweler had shown him that he was right—he said the pearls were only paste!"

161 Mrs. Guy stared at her. "Ah, I told you he wouldn't believe you."

162 "He wrote me," Charlotte continued, full of her private wrong, "that he had smashed them."

163 "He is really very disturbed." Mrs. Guy's voice

expressed pity and wonder.

164 But he was not quite clear whom she pitied, Arthur or Charlotte. And Charlotte felt disturbed, too, when she thought about it later. Had Mrs. Guy really tracked the pearls to a jeweler's window? Or had she dealt with Arthur directly? Charlotte remembered clearly that she had given Mrs. Guy his address.

PASTE
EXERCISES

A. Understanding the Plot of the Story

Answer the following questions with complete sentences.

1. Who has recently died?
2. What does Arthur ask Charlotte to do?
3. What are the "things" that Charlotte finds in her stepaunt's room? Describe them.
4. Why did Arthur's stepmother have these things?
5. What does Charlotte find in the small silk bag? What does she wonder about what she has found?
6. What does Arthur do with the jewelry? Why?
7. Why does Charlotte show the jewelry to Mrs. Guy?
8. What does Mrs. Guy tell Charlotte about the pearls?
9. What does Charlotte decide to do with the pearls?
10. What does Arthur tell Charlotte the jeweler said about the pearls?
11. In the end, where does Mrs. Guy say she got the pearls? Where else may she have got them?

PART I (PAGES 76–81)

B. Close Reading: Understanding Characterization

Central to the story in "Paste" are the personalities of Charlotte and Arthur, two of the three main characters. Henry James gives us many clues to their personalities, and in this exercise you will identify and discuss them.

1. Charlotte
   a. What is Charlotte's situation in life? What work does she do? Why does she do this work?
   b. Which of the following words best describes Charlotte's character: distrustful, thoughtful, playful? Support your choice with evidence from the first two pages of the story.
   c. Does Charlotte seem eager to find fault, or eager to please? Support your answer with evidence from the conversation between Charlotte and Arthur in paragraphs 5-60.

2. Arthur

a. What was Arthur's father's profession? What was Arthur's stepmother's profession before she married his father? What is Arthur's feeling about his stepmother?

b. What do the following quotations from the story tell about Arthur's character?

"... Charlotte had noticed that her cousin seemed somehow to grieve without sorrow, to suffer without pain." (paragraph 3)

"He looked at Charlotte for agreement, and added, like one who is unfamiliar with generosity, 'And if they're worth anything at all—why, you're all the more welcome to them.'" (paragraph 29)

c. Arthur is sure the jewels are false. More, he *needs* to be sure they are false. Why? Study the following quotations before you answer.

"Mama wasn't *that* sort of actress." (paragraph 12)
"No, they couldn't have been a present." (paragraph 47)
"I mean that her virtue was above question." (paragraph 53)
"If the pearls were *real,* and she had hidden them all these years .... Well, I wouldn't know *what* to think!" (paragraphs 57 and 59)

C. Word Forms

In the sentence below, the verb is underlined. Write your own complete sentences about the people or situations in "Paste," using different forms of that word. The word forms, and space for the new sentences, are provided.

1. Arthur could not <u>express</u> himself strongly in words.

   a. (expression) _____

_____

b. (expressive) _____

_____

2. The jewels <u>attracted</u> Charlotte even though she guessed they were "things in the theater"—that is, paste.

a. (attraction) _____

_____

b. (attractive) _____

_____

3. Charlotte <u>apologized</u> to Arthur for suggesting that his stepmother had received the pearls as a present.

a. (apology) _____

_____

b. (apologetically) _____

_____

4. Arthur did not <u>admire</u> "things of the theater."

a. (admiration) _____

_____

b. (admiringly) _____

_____

PART II (PAGES 81–86)

D. Close Reading: Understanding Unspoken or Hidden Meaning

Like any native speakers during real conversation, Charlotte and Mrs. Guy do not always say fully what they mean. They leave part of their meaning unsaid. They know the other person will understand the thing that was not spoken. Or they hope the other person will guess it. In this exercise, you will read quotations from the story and answer questions about their unspoken meanings.

1. Mrs. Guy listened with interest. "But it must be your *cousin* who is a 'dear, kind person.' Is *he* always so 'nice' to you?"

"What do you mean?" asked Charlotte (paragraph 75)

What *does* Mrs. Guy mean? Here, even Charlotte does not immediately understand. What does Mrs. Guy *know* about the pearls that Charlotte only suspects? Why, therefore, does Mrs. Guy think that Arthur has been kind to Charlotte?

2. "But if he gave them to me because he thought they were worthless—" (paragraph 93)

Charlotte does not finish this sentence, but Mrs. Guy knows exactly what she is thinking. What is it? If the pearls are real, what does Charlotte think she should do with them, and why?

3. "Yes," [said Charlotte,] "he insisted that the pearls were paste, even after I clearly said they looked different from the other things."

"Well, then, you see!" said Mrs. Guy. (paragraph 96 and 97)

With these words—"Well, then, you see!"—Mrs. Guy tells Charlotte what she should do with the pearls. What is that?

4. "Do you mean she might have stolen them?"

"No, but she had been an actress."

"Well, then!" cried Mrs. Guy. "That's exactly how she got them." (paragraphs 101–103)

What's exactly how she got them? Mrs. Guy here is leaving a whole explanation unspoken. What is that explanation? Does she think Charlotte's aunt stole the pearls? If not, how did she get them?

5. "Then you plan to return them?"

"If I don't, I'll be a thief."

"If you do, you're a fool!" said Mrs. Guy angrily.

"Well, of the two ..." Charlotte answered faintly. (paragraphs 123–126)

Charlotte leaves the end of her sentence unspoken. But Mrs. Guy, or we, could finish it for her. What does Charlotte mean here?

6. "My dear," she [Mrs. Guy] whispered, "they're things of love!"

"Oh, dear!" cried Charlotte.

"They're things of passion!"

"Oh, heavens!" (paragraphs 137–140)

With the phrases "Oh, dear!" and "Oh, heavens!," Charlotte tells us much. What does she think about the possibility that Mrs. Guy is suggesting? Why?

E. Vocabulary

Sometimes a writer describes a character or situation using words that *overstate* or *exaggerate* the truth. A simple word can thus represent something that is not in fact very simple. Read the following sentences and consider your answers to the questions that follow.

1. Mrs. Guy "had the face of a baby, but took command like a general." (paragraph 62)

Clearly, Mrs. Guy is neither a baby or a general. James has used overstatement to give the reader a picture of Mrs. Guy. What strangeness in her character does he suggest by combining the words "baby" and "general" in his description of her? Describe Mrs. Guy using your own words. What does she look like? How does she behave with other people?

2. Mrs. Guy describes the false jewels as "larger than life! … They are just what we need. They'll give me great ideas!" (paragraph 69)

Here, Mrs. Guy's overstatement tells us about her reaction to the jewels. What does "Larger than life" mean? Why will this give Mrs. Guy "great ideas"?

3. Mrs. Guy says that the pearls "need to be worn—it wakes them up. They're alive, you see. How have these been treated? They must have been buried, ignored. They were half dead. Don't you *know* about pearls?" (paragraph 86)

Mrs. Guy here talks about the pearls in terms of sleeping and waking, life and death. What has happened to the pearls since Charlotte lent them to

Mrs. Guy? How did it happen? Do *you* know about pearls? Does James's overstatement here contain any truth?

4. "How could I have known [about pearls]?' said penniless Charlotte."

Is Charlotte actually penniless? With this exaggeration, what does James tell us about Charlotte's financial and social situation?

PART III (PAGES 86–88)

F. Writing: A Letter to Arthur, "Very Truly Yours"

Arthur has written a letter to Charlotte about the pearls (see paragraphs 159–162). He says in it that the pearls were definitely false and that Charlotte has insulted his stepmother. He says that he has smashed the pearls. Later, when Charlotte sees Mrs. Guy wearing the pearls, she knows the letter was a lie. But what is the truth? Did Arthur take the pearls to a jeweler? Did Mrs. Guy buy the pearls from the jeweler? Did she "deal directly" with Arthur? Is she telling lies, too?

Imagine that you are Charlotte. What do you feel about all this? Write a letter back to Arthur. Express yourself openly and honestly. (Remember, you have nothing to lose now by speaking your mind.) Tell Arthur what you think. Remind him that you know what has happened. Decide whether you should demand something from him, or simply suggest that he reward you for keeping silent. End the letter:

> Very truly yours,
>
> Charlotte

G. Discussion: The Ending of "Paste"

Henry James fills the final pages of "Paste" with interesting possibilities and leaves the reader to choose among them. The following questions point out some of these possibilities. What is your opinion? With one or more partners (if possible), discuss *one* of the three topics below. What conclusions do you reach? Report to the whole group.

1. Charlotte finally takes the pearls back to Arthur. She hopes he will let her keep them. Instead, he locks them in a drawer and says he will take them to a jeweler. Yet he says he is sure the jeweler will say they are false. Why, then, does he keep them? Why doesn't he let Charlotte keep them, if he's so sure?

2. When Mrs. Guy learns from Charlotte about Arthur's letter, she expresses "pity and wonder." We are told, however, that "it was not quite clear whom she pitied, Arthur, or Charlotte." What reasons might she have for pitying Arthur? What reasons might she have for pitying Charlotte?

3. What do you think about Arthur, finally? Consider: If Mrs. Guy "dealt directly" with him, and if until that moment Arthur really believed he was a virtuous and honest man, then what is he feeling about himself at the end of the story? And what do you feel about him? Were his actions influenced by what he had learned about his stepmother? Do you pity him? Are you amused by what has happened to him? Do you have a low opinion of him?

Notes:

_____

_____

_____

_____

_____

_____

_____

PAUL'S CASE

Before You Read the Story . . .

1. *A Life*

Read the paragraph about Willa Cather on page 97. It tells us that Cather wrote about two very different kinds of people. What were they? What did they have in common?

2. *The Picture*

Look at the picture on page 99. What do the faces of the men in the picture show? What does the face of the boy in the picture show? Where do you think this scene is taking place?

3. *Thinking About It . . .*

"Paul's Case" is in part about some well-known conflicts: teenager against adult, student against teacher, son against father, artist against society, the lover of freedom against the world's rules. The story takes place in the first quarter of the 20th century, but its themes are as modern as today (and as old as one or three or five thousand years ago). Of the conflicts mentioned above, can you think of one that has appeared in the news recently? Can you think of one that has been important in your own life?

4. *Scanning for a Single Word and Its Context*

Sometimes we come across a particular word or phrase that seems to contain within it an important underlying idea or concept. We scan a text (or, sometimes, several texts), looking for that word or phrase. When we find it, we stop and read.

In this exercise, you are asked to scan Part I (pages 98–101) of "Paul's Case" until you find the word *usher.* When you find it, read further until you are confident that you can write a definition of the word using words or phrases from the text, or your own words. Try to complete the exercise within three minutes.

PAUL'S CASE

adapted from the story by
WILLA CATHER

Willa Cather was born in Virginia in 1873. When she was ten, her family moved to a farm in Nebraska. Nebraska then was still only partly settled. Two of Cather's famous novels, My Antonia and O Pioneers! describe pioneer life in the Middle West. As a young woman, Cather taught English, wrote for a newspaper, and edited a magazine in Pittsburgh, Pennsylvania. Then she moved to New York to work at McClure's Magazine. Much of her later writing describes painters, writers, and theater people she met there. Although different from the farmers of her youth, these artists seemed to her a different kind of pioneer. She often wrote about characters who felt the need to withdraw from society in order to discover themselves. Willa Cather died in 1947.

I

It was Paul's afternoon to appear before his teachers at Pittsburgh High School. He had been suspended a week ago. Now he was expected to explain his bad behavior. Paul entered the teachers' room, smooth and smiling. He had outgrown his clothes a little, and the velvet collar of his overcoat looked a little worn. But there was something elegant about him. He wore a jeweled pin in his neat tie. He had a red carnation in his coat. His teachers felt his appearance did not show the right attitude toward suspension.

2 Paul was tall for his age, and very thin. His large eyes had a glassy shine. He continually flashed them at people in an artificial way. His teachers found that offensive in a boy.

3 The principal asked him why he was there. Paul answered, politely enough, that he wanted to come back to school. This was a lie, but Paul was used to lying. He needed to lie to solve his problems. Then his teachers were asked to explain his behavior in class. They spoke with such anger that it was clear that Paul's case was no ordinary case. He was offensive in class. He had a contemptuous attitude toward his teachers. They attacked him like a pack of angry dogs.

4 Through all of this, Paul stood smiling, his lips open to show his teeth. Older boys than Paul had cried at such meetings. But Paul kept on flashing his eyes around him, always smiling. When he was told that he could go, he bowed gracefully, and went out. His bow, like the offensive red carnation, only showed his contempt.

5 The art teacher said what they all felt. "I don't really believe that smile is natural. There's something artificial

about it. The boy is not strong, for one thing. There is something wrong about him."

6 His teachers left the meeting angry and unhappy. But Paul ran gracefully down the hall. He was whistling a song from the opera he was going to watch that night. He hoped some of the teachers would see how little he cared about the meeting.

7 Paul worked as an usher at Carnegie Hall. Since he was late that evening he decided to go straight to the concert hall. He was always excited while he got dressed in the usher's uniform. The uniform fit him better than the other boys, and he thought he looked elegant.

8 Paul was a model usher. Graceful and smiling, he ran up and down the aisles, showing people to their seats. He carried messages as though it was his greatest pleasure in life. As the theater filled, he became more and more excited. His cheeks and lips were red and his eyes flashed. It was as if the theater was a great party and Paul was the host. When the music began, Paul sat down in back. With a sigh he lost himself in the music. The first answering sigh of the violins seemed to free some wild excitement inside him. The lights danced before his eyes, and the concert hall flashed with color. Then the singer came on, and Paul forgot all about his teachers.

9 He always felt depressed after a concert. He hated to give up the excitement and color. Tonight he waited outside the hall for the singer. When she came out, he followed her across the street to the Schenley Hotel. The hotel stood large and lit up, for singers and actors and big businessmen. Paul had often hung around the hotel, watching the people go in and out. He wanted to enter that bright elegance and leave schoolteachers and problems behind him. He watched the singer pass through the shining glass doors. In that moment, Paul felt himself pass through with her. He imagined the delicious platters of food that were brought to the dining room. He could almost see the green wine bottles in shining ice-buckets, like photographs in the newspapers.

10 A cold wind rose, and it began to rain hard. Paul was surprised to find himself standing outside. His boots

were letting in water and his overcoat was wet. Rain fell between him and the lighted windows in front of him. He wondered if he would always have to stand outside in the cold, looking in. He turned and walked slowly to the bus tracks.

II

11 Half an hour later, Paul got off the bus and walked down Cordelia Street to his house. All the houses looked alike. Clerks and small businessmen lived there, and raised large families. The children went to Sunday school, and were interested in geometry. They were just as alike each other as the houses were. Paul always felt hopeless and depressed when he walked down Cordelia Street. He had the feeling of sinking into ugliness, like water closing over his head. After the excitement of this evening he couldn't bear to see his room, with its ugly yellow wallpaper. Or the cold bathroom with the dirty tub, the broken mirror. Or his father, with his hairy legs sticking out from under his nightshirt. Paul was so late tonight that his father would be angry. Paul would have to explain, and to lie. He couldn't face it. He decided that he wouldn't go in.

12 He went around to the back of the house and found a basement window open. He climbed through and dropped down to the floor. He stood there, holding his breath, afraid of the noise he had made. But he heard nothing from upstairs. He carried a box over to the furnace to keep warm. He didn't try to sleep. He was horribly afraid of rats. And suppose his father had heard him, and came down and shot him as a thief? Then again, suppose his father came down with a gun, but Paul cried out in time to save himself? His father would be horrified to think he had nearly killed him. But what if his father wished Paul *hadn't* cried out, and *hadn't* saved himself? Paul entertained himself with these thoughts until daybreak.

13 On sunny Sunday afternoons, the people of Cordelia Street sat out on their front steps, the women in their Sunday clothes. Children played in the streets while

their parents talked. The women talked about sewing and children, the men gave advice about business and the cost of things. Paul sat there listening. The men were telling stories about the rich and powerful men who were their bosses. They owned palaces in Venice. They sailed yachts on the Mediterranean. They gambled at Monte Carlo. Paul's imagination was excited at the idea of becoming boss, but he had no mind for the clerk stage.

14 After supper was over, he helped dry the dishes. Then he asked nervously if he could go to George's for help with his geometry. His father asked him why he couldn't study with someone who lived nearer. And he shouldn't leave his homework until Sunday. But finally he gave him money for the bus. Paul ran upstairs to wash the small of dishwater from his hands. He shook a few drops of cologne over his fingers. Then he left the house with his geometry book, very obvious, under his arm. The moment he left Cordelia Street and got on the bus, he shook off two days of deadening boredom. He began to live again.

15 Paul had a friend, Charley Edwards, who was a young actor. Paul spent every extra moment in Charley's dressing-room, helping him dress. It was at the theater and concert hall that Paul really lived. The rest was only a sleep and a forgetting. This was Paul's fairy tale, this was his secret love. The moment he breathed the smell behind the scenes, his imagination took fire. The moment the violins began to play, he shook off all stupid and ugly things.

16 In Paul's world, natural things were nearly always ugly. Perhaps that was why he thought artificiality was necessary to beauty. His life was full of Sunday-school picnics, saving money, good advice, and the smell of cooking. It was not that he wanted to become an actor or musician. What he wanted was to see theater, to breathe its air, to be carried away from it all.

17 After a night behind the scenes, Paul found school worse than ever. He hated the bare floors and empty walls. He hated the teachers: boring men who never wore carnations in their old suits. And he hated the women, with

their dull dresses and high voices, who spoke so seriously about prepositions and adjectives. He couldn't bear to have the other students think he took these people seriously. He wanted them to see that school meant nothing to him. It was all a joke. He showed his classmates pictures of his friends at the theater. He told them unbelievable stories of his midnight suppers with actors and musicians. He talked about the flowers he sent to his actor friends, and the trips they would take together.

18 Things went worse and worse at school. Paul was offensive to the teachers. He had no time for geometry, he was too busy helping his friends at the theater. Finally the principal went to Paul's father. Paul was taken out of school. He was put to work as a clerk for Denny & Carson. The manager of Carnegie Hall was told to get another usher. The doorman at the theater was told not to let him in. Charley Edwards promised not to see him again. The theater people were amused when they heard the stories Paul had told. They agreed that Paul was a bad case.

III

19 The train ran east through a January snowstorm. Paul woke up as the train whistled outside of New York City. He felt dirty and uncomfortable. He had taken the night train to avoid any Pittsburgh businessman who might have seen him at Denny & Carson.

20 When he arrived at the station he took a taxi to a large men's store. He spent two hours there, buying carefully: a suit, dress clothes, shirts and silk underwear. He drove on to a hat shop and a shoe shop. His last stop was at Tiffany's, where he chose silver brushes and a tie-pin. Then he had the taxi take him to the Waldorf Hotel.

21 When he was shown into his rooms on the eighth floor, he saw that everything was as it should be. Only one thing was missing. He ordered flowers brought up to his room. Outside the snow was falling wildly, but inside the air was soft and smelled of flowers. He was very tired. He had been in such a hurry, and had been under such pressure.

He had come so far in the last 24 hours.

22 It had been wonderfully simple. When they shut him out of the theater and the concert hall, the whole thing was sure to happen. It was only a matter of when. The only thing that surprised Paul was his own courage. He had always been afraid. Even when he was a little boy he felt fear watching him from a dark corner. And Paul had done things that were not pretty to watch, he knew. But now he felt free of that—he had driven fear away.

23 Only yesterday he had been sent to the bank with Denny & Carson's money. There was more than two thousand dollars in checks, and nearly a thousand in cash. He had slipped the thousand into his pocket, and left only the checks at the bank. He knew no one would notice for two or three days, and his father was away on business for the week. From the time he slipped the money into his pocket, and caught the train to New York, he had never lost his nerve.

24 When he woke up it was four o'clock. He dressed carefully and took a taxi up Fifth Avenue to Central Park. Snow fell against shop windows full of spring flowers. The park looked like a winter scene in the theater. Later, at dinner, he sat alone at a table near the window. The flowers, the white table-cloths, the many-colored wine glasses, the bright dresses of the women, the low music of the violins—all these things filled him with joy. Paul wondered why there were any honest men at all—this was what all the world was fighting for. He couldn't believe in Cordelia Street. He felt only contempt for those people. Had he ever lived there? Alone later, at the opera, he was not lonely. He had no wish to meet or know any of these elegant people. All he wanted was the right to be a part of the scene and watch.

25 The manager of the hotel was not suspicious. Paul drew no attention to himself. His pleasures were quiet ones. He loved to sit in the evenings in his living room. He enjoyed his flowers, his clothes, his cigarette, and his feeling of power. He could not remember a time when he had been so at peace with himself. He was glad not to have to lie, day after day. He had only lied to make people notice

him. He wanted to prove his difference from the boys on Cordelia Street. Now he could be honest. He felt no guilt at what he had done. His golden days went by without a shadow. He made each one as perfect as he could.

26 On the eighth day after his arrival in New York, he saw the whole story in the Pittsburgh paper. The company of Denny & Carson reported that the boy's father had paid back what he stole. They would not send Paul to jail. His father thought he might be in New York. He was on his way East to find his son.

27 Paul felt terrible. The thought of returning to Cordelia Street, to Sunday school, to his ugly room, to old dishtowels, was worse than jail. He had the terrible feeling that the music had stopped, the play was over. But later, at dinner, the violin and the flash of light and color had their old magic. He drank his wine wildly. He would show himself that he could finish the game with elegance. Was he not a very special person? Wasn't this the world where he belonged?

28 The next morning he woke up with a headache. He had never felt so depressed. Yet somehow he was not afraid. Perhaps he had looked into the dark corner where his terror had always waited. He saw everything clearly now. He had the feeling that he had made the best of it. He had lived the sort of life he was meant to live.

29 Paul took a taxi out into the country. Then he sent the taxi away and walked along the train tracks. The snow lay heavy on the ground. He climbed a little hill above the tracks, and sat down. He noticed that the carnations in his coat were dying in the cold. All the flowers he had seen that first night in New York must have gone the same way. They only had one bright breath of life. It was a losing game, it seemed, to fight against the world's advice. Paul took one of the carnations from his coat. He dug a hole in the snow and carefully covered up the flower.

30 The sound of a train brought him back. He jumped to his feet, afraid that he might be too late. He was smiling nervously. His eyes moved left and right, as if someone was watching him. When the right moment came, he jumped.

As he fell, he saw with regret all that he had left undone. The blue Mediterranean, the gold of Monte Carlo. He felt something hit his chest. His body was thrown through the air, on and on, further and faster. Then, his imagination flashed into black, and Paul dropped back into the immense design of things.

PAUL'S CASE
EXERCISES

A. Understanding the Plot of the Story

Answer the following questions with complete sentences.

1. Why does Paul have to come back to school one afternoon?
2. Why are his teachers angry with him?
3. Where does Paul go after the meeting? What is his job there?
4. What does Paul think about his neighborhood, Cordelia Street? What is his feeling about the world of the theater and concert hall?
5. Why is he taken out of school? What is he forced to do?
6. Where does Paul run away to? What does he do there?
7. How does he pay for the trip?
8. What happens to Paul after he reads the newspaper that tells what he has done?

PART I (PAGES 98–101)

B. Close Reading and Vocabulary

Choose words from the following list that fit the blank spaces in the statements below. Then write answers to the questions that follow the statements.

gracefully	suspension	flash	elegance
artificial	contempt	offensive	attitude

1. Paul's _____ from school lasted one week. What had he done to deserve that punishment?

_____

_____

2. Paul's teachers did not like Paul's _____ toward being suspended. In particular, what did they object to

in Paul's behavior toward them in the meeting?

_____

_____

3. Paul's attitude toward life could be seen in the jeweled pin in his neat tie—a touch of _____. What other such sign did he present to the world?

_____

_____

4. Paul's teachers didn't find his red carnation elegant. On the contrary, they found it _____. What did they do as a result?

_____

_____

5. Paul offended his teachers in class because he obviously was not interested in his lessons, and they saw this disinterest as a sign of _____. Yet when asked if he wanted to come back to school, what did he answer? Why?

_____

_____

6. To his teachers, Paul's contemptuous attitude was obvious from his clothes, from his manner, and certainly from the way he _____ his eyes at them. Do you think Paul behaved this way consciously—on purpose? Why, or why not?

_____

_____

7. Paul's smile, flashing eyes, open mouth, little bow at the end—these things, far from being natural, were completely _____. Did his teachers see this as a sign of strength or weakness? Why?

_____

_____

8. In the theater—that place of total artifice—Paul felt completely natural, completely at home, and moved _____up and down the aisles. In fact, how important was the role that he played at the concert hall?

_____

_____

C. Word Forms

In the exercise below, re-write each sentence, expressing the same meaning but using a different form of the word that is underlined. The new word form is given in parentheses. You may have to add or subtract words as well as rearrange words in the sentences.

1. At the meeting Paul's teachers <u>expected</u> him to explain his bad behavior.

(expectation) _____

_____

2. Paul was <u>graceful</u> as he ran up and down the aisles of the theater.

(gracefully)_____

_____

3. As the theater filled, his cheeks and lips were red, and his eyes flashed with <u>excitement</u>.

(excitedly)_____

_____

4. Paul always felt <u>depressed</u> in the moments just after a concert or opera.

(depressing)_____

_____

5. He <u>imagined</u> delicious platters of food, shining bottles of wine.

(imagination)_____

_____

PART II (PAGES 101–103)

D. Close Reading: Cordelia Street

In Part II, Cather is careful to show us the contrast in Paul's mind between the real world of his neighborhood, Cordelia Street, and the dream world of the theater and concert hall. In this exercise, you are asked to recall the details that make up Cather's picture of Cordelia Street.

1. "In Paul's world, natural things were nearly always ugly." (paragraph 16). Re-read paragraph 11, and then list eight things about Cordelia Street that Paul found ugly, boring, or depressing.

2. Where did Paul spend the night? *How* did he spent the night? Why did he spend it that way?

3. Paragraph 13 introduces us to the people of Cordelia Street. Who are they? What kind of jobs do they hold? What do they talk about when they gather on their front steps?

4. Before he leaves his house, how does Paul "get rid" of the feel of Cordelia Street?

5. When Paul is removed from school, what four things happen that remove him further from the world he loves and push him closer to the world he hates? (paragraph 18)

E. Language Activity: Interview, "Fairy Tales and Secret Loves"

Look again at what Cather tells us about the world of the theater and concert hall in Paul's mind:

> This was Paul's fairy tale, this was his secret love. The moment he breathed the smell behind the scenes, his imagination took fire. The moment the violins began to play, he shook off all stupid and ugly things.

In this exercise, you are asked to interview a young person, aged 15–19. You want to find what it is that allows this person to "shake off all stupid or ugly things." Report the results of your interview to the whole class.
During the interview, you may want to ask some of the following questions:

• What do you do when you want to forget your problems?

• Is there a particular place you can go where your problems disappear, or where you feel you can be yourself?

• What activity makes you feel most happy, relaxed, at home?

• What activity allows you to feel most free from other people's expectations of you?

• Do you feel most natural when you are completely alone, when you are alone in a crowd, or when you are with friends? Why do you think this is so?

• Do you ever, in your imagination, think about a career that you know you may not actually be able to have in real life? What is that career? Are you sure you won't try for it?

• Do other people you know have secret dreams, secret loves? What is the strangest one you know of?

PART III (PAGES 103–106)

F. Writing: A Personal Narrative

Choose *one* of the two topics below for a composition. Write 350–500 words.

1. In Part III of "Paul's Case," Willa Cather is careful to show us many details of Paul's life as he realizes his deepest wish: to live a life of complete freedom in elegant surroundings. The details of Paul's brief triumph are memorable: his new clothes, the silver brushes, the elegant rooms at the Waldorf Hotel, the flowers, a night at the opera. And we are told: "Paul drew no attention to himself. His pleasures were quiet ones." In fact, Paul realizes his dream completely, if briefly.

   Now, using your own experience—or the experience of the person you interviewed in Exercise G, or the experience of someone you know, or an experience out of your imagination—describe another case of someone realizing a deep wish. The moment of fulfillment may have been brief. But describe it fully, using details that will bring that moment alive for your reader. You may write in the first person ("I") or the third person ("he" or "she").

2. "It was a losing game, it seemed, to fight against the world's advice." This is Paul's conclusion after his brief, momentary victory.

   Drawing again on your own experience, or on your imagination, or on the experience of someone you know, describe an attempt to "fight against the world's advice" that failed. What were the circumstances? Why did the attempt fail? What were the results of the failure? What were the person's feelings in the end? Write in the first person or third person ("he" or "she").

G. Discussion: Paul's Case

1. How did you feel about the ending of the story? Were you surprised? shocked? saddened? Did you feel that

the ending had to happen the way it did? What other path might Paul have taken? Would that path have been within his nature, as we came to know it in the story?

2. What is the meaning, in your opinion, of the final phrase: "… and Paul dropped back into the immense design of things." *Immense* means huge, unable to be measured. A *design* is a plan, or the working out of a plan: a project with a purpose or aim. Thus the phrase "immense design of things" is almost a contradiction: a plan so big we cannot measure it or understand it. Does this idea help us understand or accept Paul's death? Why, or why not? How, in the end, did the story make you feel?

3. The word "case" in the story's title is an interesting one. It means situation or condition; and it also means a special example or problem. In other words, we know from the start that the "Paul" of the title will be no ordinary young man. But how special is he? Do you think Paul's "case" is so unusual as to be unrealistic? Can you think of other "cases" that in some way are similar to Paul's? Do you think modern society produces more or fewer such cases than the society of 75–100 years ago?

Notes:

_____

_____

_____

_____

_____

_____

_____

_____

THE LOST PHOEBE

Before You Read the Story ...

1. *A Life*

The paragraph about Theodore Dreiser on page 115 mentions two important difficulties his family faced when he was a child. What were they? How would you expect these to influence his writing?

2. *The Picture*

Look at the picture on page 125. Where is the man walking? What time of day is it? What do you notice about his appearance? What conclusions do you draw from the way he looks?

3. *Thinking About It ...*

In this story Dreiser writes about a family in a small rural community a century ago. Most people in such communities kept small farms then. Their lives followed a certain pattern according to their work. There wasn't much time, money, or opportunity for making changes in life style. What effect would this have on how people lived? On their relationship to their neighbors? On how people expected them to behave? Have things changed today? In what ways? Do most people you know do the same work, or hold the same job, all their lives? Are they close to their neighbors? Do they expect, or allow, a wide difference in personality and behavior?

4. *Scanning to get the Basic Idea*

Sometimes we scan a lengthy piece of writing in order to get the basic idea of the whole piece. We may or may not need, or want, to return to the beginning and read with care all the way through. In this exercise, you are asked to scan the entire story of "The Lost Phoebe" and answer questions on the story's basic idea.

In order to do this, scan the story, reading the first sentence or two of each paragraph. Read no more than that, but do not rush. When you come to a long section of dialogue, let your eyes wander down the page, and try to get a general impression of the dialogue. When you are finished, turn to Exercise A on page 129 and *write down* answers to as many of the questions as you can. Scan the story a second time, looking only for answers to the questions you couldn't answer the first time. Try to complete the first scanning in five minutes, and the writing in another five.

THE LOST PHOEBE

adapted from the story by
THEODORE DREISER

Theodore Dreiser was born in 1871. When he was a child, his family was poor—so poor, in fact, that his mother and father had to separate from each other in order to support the children. With his mother and two of his sisters, Dreiser lived in many different towns and states. Although he spent only one year at college, Dreiser became a journalist and magazine editor. His first novel, Sister Carrie, was published in 1901. The book was not well liked at first, partly because the "good" men in the story were not always rewarded nor the "bad" men always punished. Dreiser was one of the leaders of the "naturalist" school in American writing. He tried to record with great honesty and accuracy exactly what he saw. His writing was not always beautiful on the surface, but its depth was remarkable from the beginning. Dreiser's most famous novel was An American Tragedy, one of the most influential novels in American fiction. It was published in 1925. Dreiser died in 1945.

I

Old Henry Reifsneider and his wife Phoebe had lived together for forty-eight years. They had lived three miles from a small town whose population was steadily falling. This part of the country was not as wealthy as it used to be. It wasn't thickly settled, either. Perhaps there was a house every mile or so, with fields in between. Their own house had been built by Henry's grandfather many years ago. A new part had been added to the original log cabin when Henry married Phoebe. The new part was now weatherbeaten. Wind whistled through cracks in the boards. Large, lovely trees surrounded the house. But they made it seem a little damp inside.

2 The furniture, like the house, was old. There was a tall cupboard of cherry-wood and a large, old-fashioned bed. The chest of drawers was also high and wide and solidly built. But it had faded, and smelled damp. The carpet that lay under the strong, lasting furniture had been made by Phoebe herself, fifteen years before she died. Now it was worn and faded to a dull grey and pink. The frame that she had made the carpet on was still there. It stood like a dusty, bony skeleton in the east room. All sorts of broken-down furniture lay around the place. There was a doorless clothes-cupboard. A broken mirror hung in an old cherry-wood frame. It had fallen from a nail and cracked three days before their youngest son, Jerry, died. There was a hat-stand whose china knobs had broken off. And an old-fashioned sewing machine.

3 The orchard to the east of the house was full of rotting apple trees. Their twisted branches were covered with greenish-white moss which looked sad and ghostly in the moonlight. Besides the orchard, several low buildings

surrounded the house. They had once housed chickens, a horse or two, a cow, and several pigs. The same grey-green moss covered their roofs. They had not been painted for so long that they had turned a greyish-black. In fact, everything on the farm had aged and faded along with Old Henry and his wife Phoebe.

4 They had lived here, these two, since their marriage forty-eight years before. And Henry had lived here as a child. His father and mother had been old when Henry married. They had invited him to bring his wife to the farm. They had all lived together for ten years before his mother and father died. After that Henry and Phoebe were left alone with their four children. But all sorts of things had happened since then. They had had seven children, but three had died. One girl had gone to Kansas. One boy had gone to Sioux Falls and was never even heard from again. Another boy had gone to Washington. The last girl lived five counties away in the same state. She had so many problems of her own, however, that she rarely gave her parents a thought. Their very ordinary home life had never been attractive to the children. So time had drawn them away. Wherever they were, they gave little thought to their father and mother.

5 Old Henry Reifsneider and his wife Phoebe were a loving couple. You perhaps know how it is with such simple people. They fasten themselves like moss on stones, until they and their circumstances are worn away. The larger world has no call to them; or if it does, they don't hear it. The orchard, the fields, the pigpen and the chicken house measure the range of their human activities. When the wheat is ripe, it is harvested. When the corn is full, it is cut. After that comes winter. The grain is taken to market, the wood is cut for the fires. The work is simple: fire-building, meal-getting, occasional repairing, visiting. There are also changes in the weather—the snow, the rains, and the fair days. Beyond these things, nothing else means very much. All the rest of life is a far-off dream. It shines, far away, like starlight. It sounds as faint as cowbells in the distance.

6 Old Henry and his wife Phoebe were as fond of each

other as it is possible for two old people who have nothing else in this life to be fond of. He was a thin old man, seventy when she died. He was a strange, moody person with thick, uncombed grey-black hair and beard. He looked at you out of dull, fish-like watery eyes. His clothes, like the clothes of many farmers, were old and ill-fitting. They were too large at the neck. The knees and elbows were stretched and worn. Phoebe was thin and shapeless. She looked like an umbrella, dressed in black. As time had passed they had only themselves to look after. Their activities had become fewer and fewer. The herd of pigs was reduced to one. The sleepy horse Henry still kept was neither very clean nor well-fed. Almost all the chickens had disappeared. They had been killed by animals or disease. The once-healthy vegetable garden was now only a memory of itself. The flower beds were overgrown. A will had been made which divided the small property equally among the remaining four children. It was so small that it was really of no interest to any of them. Yet Henry and Phoebe lived together in peace and sympathy. Once in a while Old Henry would become moody and annoyed. He would complain that something unimportant had been lost.

7 "Phoebe, where's my corn knife? You never leave my things alone."

8 "Now you be quiet, Henry," his wife would answer in her old cracked voice. "If you don't, I'll leave you. I'll get up and walk out of here one day. Then where would you be? You don't have anybody but me to look after you, so just behave yourself. Your corn knife is in the cupboard where it's always been, unless you put it somewhere else."

9 Old Henry knew his wife would never leave him. But sometimes he wondered what he would do if she died. That was the one leaving he was afraid of. Every night he wound the old clock and went to lock the doors, and it comforted him to know Phoebe was in bed. If he moved in his sleep she would be there to ask him what he wanted.

10 "Now, Henry, do lie still! You're as restless as a chicken."

11 "Well, I can't sleep, Phoebe."

12 "Well, you don't have to roll over so much. You can let *me* sleep." This would usually put him to sleep.

13 If she wanted a pail of water, he complained, but it gave him pleasure to bring it. If she rose first to build the fire, he made sure the wood was cut and placed within easy reach. So they divided this simple world nicely between them.

II

14 In the spring of her sixty-fourth year, Phoebe became sick. Old Henry drove to town and brought back the doctor. But because of her age, her sickness was not curable, and one cold night she died. Henry could have gone to live with his youngest daughter. But it was really too much trouble. He was too weary and used to his home. He wanted to remain near where they had put his Phoebe.

15 His neighbors invited him to stay with them. But he didn't want to. So his friends left him with advice and offers of help. They sent supplies of coffee and bacon and bread. He tried to interest himself in farming to keep himself busy. But it was sad to come into the house in the evening. He could find no shadow of Phoebe, although everything in the house suggested her. At night he read the newspapers that friends had left for him. Or he read in his Bible, which he had forgotten about for years. But he could get little comfort from these things. Mostly he sat and wondered where Phoebe had gone, and how soon he would die.

16 He made coffee every morning and fried himself some bacon at night. But he wasn't hungry. His house was empty; its shadows saddened him. So he lived quite unhappily for five long months. And then a change began.

17 It was a moonlight night. The moss-covered orchard shone ghostly silver. As usual, Henry was thinking of Phoebe and the years they had been young together. And he thought about the children who had gone. The condition of the house was becoming worse. The sheets were not clean, because he made a poor job of the laundry. The roof leaked, and things inside got damp. But he didn't

do anything about it. He preferred to walk slowly back and forth, or sit and think.

18 By 12:00 midnight of this particular night, however, he was asleep. He woke up at 2:00. The moon shone in through the living room windows. His coat lying on the back of the chair made a shadow near the table. It looked like Phoebe as she used to sit there. Could it be she—or her ghost? He never used to believe in spirits, and yet ... He stared at it in the pale light. His old hair seemed to rise up from his head. He sat up, but the figure did not move. He put his thin legs out of the bed. He wondered if this could really be Phoebe. They had often talked about ghosts and spirits. But they had never agreed that such things could be. His wife had never believed that her spirit could return to walk the earth. She had believed in a heaven where good folk would want to stay and not come back. Yet here she was now, bending over the table. She was wearing her black dress. Her face shone pale in the moonlight.

19 "Phoebe," he called, excited from head to toe. "Have you come back?"

20 The figure did not move. He got up and walked uncertainly towards the door, watching it carefully. As he came near, however, the ghost became once more his coat upon the chair.

21 "Well," he said to himself, his mouth open in wonder, "I surely thought I saw her." He ran his hands through his hair while his excitement relaxed. Although it had disappeared, he had the idea that she might return.

22 Another night he looked out of the window toward the chicken house and pigpen. Mist was rising from the damp ground, and he thought he saw Phoebe. She always used to cross from the kitchen door to the pigpen to feed the pigs. And here she was again. He sat up and watched her. He was doubtful because of the first experience. But his body shook with excitement. Perhaps there really were spirits. Phoebe must be worried about his loneliness. She must be thinking about him. He watched her until a breath of wind blew the mist away.

23 A third night, as he was dreaming, she came to his bed.

24 "Poor Henry," she said. "It's too bad." He woke up and thought he saw her move from the bedroom into the living room. He got up, greatly astonished. He was sure that Phoebe was coming back to him. If he thought about her enough, if he showed her how much he needed her, she would come back. She would tell him what to do. Perhaps she would stay with him most of the time. At least, during the night. That would make him less lonely.

25 For the old or weak, imagination may easily develop into actual hallucination. Eventually this change happened for Henry. Night after night he waited, expecting her return. Once in a strange mood he thought he saw a pale light moving about the room. Another time he saw her walking in the orchard after dark. Then one morning he felt he could not bear his loneliness any longer. He woke up with the knowledge that she was not dead. It is hard to say how he felt so certain. His mind was gone. In its place was the hallucination that he and Phoebe had had a senseless quarrel. He had complained that she had moved his pipe. In the past she had jokingly threatened to leave him if he did not behave himself.

26 "I guess I could find you again," he had always said. But her joking threat had always been the same:

27 "You won't find me if I ever leave you. I guess I can get to some place where you can't find me."

28 When he got up that morning he didn't build the fire or cut the bread as usual. He began to think where he should look for her. He put on his soft hat and took his walking-stick from behind the door. He started out energetically to look for her among his neighbors. His old shoes scratched loudly in the dust. His grey hair, now grown rather long, hung down below his hat. His hands and face were pale.

29 "Why, hello, Henry! Where are you going this morning?" inquired Farmer Dodge.

30 "You haven't seen Phoebe, have you?"

31 "Phoebe who?" asked Farmer Dodge. He didn't connect the name with Henry's dead wife.

32 "Why, my wife, Phoebe, of course. Who do you

suppose I mean?"

33 "Oh, come on, Henry! You aren't joking, are you? It can't be your wife you're talking about. She's dead."

34 "Dead? Not Phoebe! She left me early this morning while I was sleeping. We had a little quarrel last night, and I guess that's the reason. But I guess I can find her. She's gone over to Matilda Race's, that's where she's gone."

35 He started quickly up the road. The astonished Dodge stared after him. "Well!" he said to himself. "He's gone crazy. That poor old man has lived down there alone until he's gone completely out of his mind. I'll have to inform the police."

36 "Why, Mr. Reifsneider," cried old Matilda Race as Henry knocked on her door. "What brings you here this morning?"

37 "Is Phoebe here?" he demanded eagerly.

38 "Phoebe who? What Phoebe?" replied Mrs. Race, curious.

39 "Why, my Phoebe, of course, my wife Phoebe. Who do you suppose? Isn't she here now?"

40 "Why, you poor man!" cried Mrs. Race. "You've lost your mind. You come right in and sit down. I'll get you a cup of coffee. Of course your wife isn't here. But you come in and sit down. I'll find her for you after a while. I know where she is."

41 The old farmer's eyes softened at her sympathy.

42 "We had a quarrel last night and she left me," Henry offered.

43 "Oh, my!" Mrs. Race sighed to herself. There was no one there to share her astonishment. "The poor man! Now somebody's just got to look after him. He can't be allowed to run around the country this way looking for his dead wife. It's terrible."

44 She boiled him a pot of coffee and brought in some new-baked bread and fresh butter. She put on a couple of eggs to boil, lying as she spoke:

45 "Now, you stay right there, Henry, until Jake comes in. I'll sent him to look for Phoebe. I think she must be over at Sumnerton with some of her friends. Anyhow, we'll

find out. Now you just drink this coffee and eat this bread. You must be tired. You've had a long walk this morning." Her idea was to wait for her husband, Jake, and perhaps have him call the police.

46 Henry ate, but his mind was on his wife. Since she was not here, perhaps she was visiting the Murrays—miles away in another direction. He decided that he would not wait for Jake Race. He would search for his wife himself.

47 "Well, I'll be going," he said, getting up and looking strangely about him. "I guess she didn't come here after all. She went over to the Murrays', I guess." And he marched out, ignoring Matilda Race's cries of worry.

48 Two hours later his dusty, eager figure appeared in the Murrays' doorway. He had walked five miles and it was noon. The Murrays, a husband and wife of sixty, listened to him with astonishment. They also realized that he was mad. They invited him to stay to dinner. They intended to call the police later, to see what could be done. But Henry did not stay long. His need for Phoebe pulled him off to another distant farmhouse. So it went for that day and the next and the next. And the circle of his questioning grew wider and wider.

49 And although Henry came to many doors, and the police were informed, it was decided not to send him to the county hospital. The condition of mad patients in this hospital was horrifying. It was found that Henry returned peaceably to his lonely home at night to see if his wife had returned. Who would lock up a thin, eager, old man with grey hair and a kindly, innocent, inquiring manner? His neighbors had known him as a kindly, dependable man. He could do no harm. Many people gave him food and old clothes—at least at first. His figure became a common sight, and the answer, "Why no, Henry, I haven't seen her," or, "No, Henry, she hasn't been here today," became more customary.

III

50 For several years afterward he was an odd figure in the sun and rain, on dusty roads and muddy ones. The longer he walked in this manner the deeper his strange hallucination became. He found it harder and harder to return from his more and more distant searches. Finally he began to take a few eating utensils with him so he would not have to return home at night. In an old coffeepot he put a small tin cup. He took a knife, fork, and spoon, and salt and pepper. He tied a tin plate to the pot. It was no trouble for him to get the little food he needed. And with a strange, almost religious manner, he didn't hesitate to ask for that much. Slowly his hair became longer and longer. His black hat became an earthen brown, and his clothes worn and dusty.

51 For three years he walked with only his clothes, his stick, and his utensils. No one knew how far he went, or how he lived through the storms and cold. They did not see him find shelter in piles of grass or by the sides of cattle. The warm bodies of the cows protected him from cold, and their dull minds did not oppose his presence. Overhanging rocks and trees kept him from the rain.

52 The progress of such hallucinations is strange. He had asked for Phoebe at people's doors and got no answer. Finally he decided that she was not in any of the houses. But she might be within reach of his voice. So he began to call sad, occasional cries. "O-o-o Phoebe! O-o-o Phoebe!" waked the quiet countryside and echoed through the hills. It had a sad, mad ring. Many farmers recognized it from far away and said, "There goes old Reifsneider."

53 Sometimes when he reached a crossroad, he couldn't decide which way to go. He developed another hallucination to help him. He believed Phoebe's spirit or some power of the air or wind or nature would tell him where to go. He would stand at the crossroad and close his eyes. He would turn around three times and call "O-o-o Phoebe" twice. Then he would throw his walking stick

straight before him. This would surely tell him which way to go. Phoebe or some magic power would direct the stick. He would then follow the direction the stick pointed, even when it led him back the way he had come. And the hallucination that he would surely find her remained. There were hours when his feet were sore and his legs tired. There were times when he would stop in the heat to wipe his forehead, or in the cold to beat his arms. Sometimes, after throwing his stick and finding it pointing to where he had just come from, he would shake his head wearily and philosophically. He would consider for a moment the confusion and disappointment of life, and his own strange fate. Then he would start energetically off again. His strange figure finally became known in the farthest corners of three or four counties. Old Reifsneider was a sad character. His fame was wide.

54 About four miles from the little town called Watersville there was a place called Red Cliff. This cliff was a steep wall of red sandstone, perhaps a hundred feet high. It rose above the fruitful corn fields and orchards that lay beneath. Trees grew thickly along the top of the cliff. In fair weather it was old Reifsneider's habit to spend the night here. He would fry his bacon or boil his eggs at the foot of some tree. Then he would lie down.

55 He almost always woke at 2:00 in the morning. Occasionally he would walk at night. More often he would sit up and watch the darkness or the stars, wondering. Sometimes in the strangeness of his mind he imagined he saw his lost wife moving among the trees. Then he would get up to follow. He would take his utensils on a string, and his stick. When she tried to escape him he would run after her, begging. When she disappeared he would feel disappointed. He was saddened at the almost impossible difficulties of his search.

56 One night in the seventh year of his search he came to the top of Red Cliff. It was spring, like the spring when Phoebe had died. He had walked many many miles with his utensils, following his walking stick. It was after 10:00 at night. He was very tired. Long walking and little

eating had left him only a shadow of his former self. He had little strength. Only his hallucination kept him going. He had eaten hardly anything that day. Now, exhausted, he lay down in the dark to rest and possibly sleep.

57 He felt the presence of his wife strongly. It would not be long now until he should see her, talk to her, he told himself. He fell asleep, after a time, his head on his knees. At midnight the moon began to rise. At 2:00 in the morning, his wakeful hour, it was a large silver ball. He opened his eyes. The moonlight made silvery patterns at his feet. The forest was full of strange light and silvery, shadowy forms. What was it that moved among the trees—a pale, shining, ghostly figure? Moonlight and shadow gave it a strange form and a stranger reality. Was it truly his lost Phoebe? It came near him. He imagined he could see her eyes. Not as she was when he last saw her in the black dress and shawl. Now she was a strangely younger Phoebe. She was the one whom he had known years before as a girl. Old Reifsneider got up. He had been expecting and dreaming of this hour all these years. Now he saw the pale light dancing before him. He looked at it questioningly, one hand on his grey hair.

58 For the first time in many years he suddenly remembered the full beauty of the girlish form. He saw her pleasing, sympathetic smile, her brown hair. He remembered the blue ribbon she had once worn about her waist. He saw her light and happy movements. He forgot his pots and pans and followed her. She moved before him and it seemed that she waved to him with a young and playful hand.

59 "Oh, Phoebe! Phoebe!" he called. "Have you really come? Have you really answered me?" On and on he hurried until he was almost running. He brushed his arms against the trees. He struck his hands and face against small branches. His hat was gone, his breath was gone, his mind quite gone when he came to the edge of the cliff. Down below he saw her among the silver apple trees now blooming in the spring.

60 "Oh, Phoebe!" he called. "Oh, Phoebe! Oh no,

don't leave me!" He felt the pull of the world where love was young and Phoebe waited. "Oh, wait, Phoebe!" he cried, and jumped.

61 Some farm boys found his utensils under the tree where he had left them. Later, at the foot of the cliff, they found his body. He was pale and broken, but full of happiness. A smile of peace curved is lips. His old hat was discovered under a tree. No one of all the simple population knew how eagerly and happily he had finally found his lost Phoebe.

THE LOST PHOEBE
EXERCISES

A. Understanding the Plot of the Story

Answer the following questions with complete sentences.

1. How long had Henry and Phoebe been married?
2. Had their marriage been a happy or an unhappy one?
3. What is their relationship to their neighbors? To their children? To the rest of the world generally?
4. What does Henry imagine he sees, after Phoebe dies?
5. Why does Henry leave home? How would you describe his behavior as he walks all over the countryside?
6. How long does he continue to search for Phoebe?
7. What happens to Henry on the top of Red Cliff?

PART I (PAGES 116–119)
B. Close Reading: Understanding Important Details

A story's sense of reality comes from the small but important details included by the writer. In Part I of "The Lost Phoebe," Dreiser wants us to understand Henry Reifsneider's situation exactly, and he does this by carefully presenting the important details of Henry's life. Do you remember them? If not, can you find them?

1. When was the "new part" of Henry's house added to the original log cabin? (paragraph 1) What did this "new part" look like now?
2. Eight pieces of furniture are mentioned. What are they? Which two pieces give us information about two members of Henry's family?
3. What covered both the roof of the buildings and the trees of the orchard?
4. Which sentence in paragraph 3 summarizes the condition of Old Henry's farm?
5. Henry and Phoebe had seven children. What became of each of these children?
6. What activities filled the lives of Henry and Phoebe? List at least six.

C. Language Activity: Figurative Language

If a story's sense of reality comes from its details, the atmosphere of a story comes from the writer's use of language. Figurative language is the use of words to create meaningful pictures in the reader's mind. Below are examples of, and questions about, Dreiser's use of figurative language.

Working with a partner (if possible), answer the questions below, and add your own examples of figurative language as requested.

1. The frame for making carpets stood "like a dusty bony skeleton in the east room." (paragraph 2) What does this phrase tell us about the frame? about the general appearance of the east room? Picture a piece of furniture in your own room, apartment, or house. What can you compare it to (what is it *like?*) that will help others see it, and get a sense of the whole room?

2. The twisted branches of the apple trees were covered with moss. and we are told that they looked "ghostly" in the moonlight (paragraph 3). What mood or character does Dreiser give to the apple orchard with this one word? Think of another kind of tree, or group of trees, and describe them with a word, or words, that has nothing to do with tree trunks, leaves, or branches. See if your partner, or classmates, can guess what kind of tree you are describing.

3. The life of the world outside the farm is, to the Reifsneiders, like a "far-off dream ... it shines, far away, like starlight ... it sounds as faint as cowbells in the distance." (paragraph 5) In trying to describe this outside world, Dreiser tells us how it feels (like a dream), what it looks like (faraway starlight), and what it sounds like (faint as distant cowbells). With these phrases in mind, tell in your own words what the "outside" world means to the Reifsneiders. Then think of a place, town, city, or country you know, and say what it feels like, looks like, and sounds like.

4. Henry's eyes are "fish-like"; Phoebe looks like "an umbrella." With only these words in mind, use your own words to describe Henry's and Phoebe's *personalities*. Then think of a famous person whose face is generally known, and with a single word or phrase, give a sense of what that person looks like, and perhaps a sense of his or her personality as well.

5. What does Phoebe mean when she says that Henry is "as restless as a chicken"? (paragraph 10) Then use the same kind of phrase—as (adjective) as a (kind of animal)—to describe your best friend, worst enemy, or someone in your family.

PART II (PAGES 119–123)

D. Vocabulary and Word Forms

Part II contains many words that express or suggest strong emotion. You may not be accustomed to using all the forms of these words, and in this exercise you are asked to fill in the blanks with the less common form of the word given in parentheses.

(sad) saddened	(wonder) wondering
(hallucination) hallucinatory	(crazy) crazed
(mad) maddeningly	(astonish) astonishment
(sympathetic) sympathetically	(quarrel) quarrelsome

1. Henry felt the presence of his wife strongly; yet she remained _____ out of sight, beyond his reach.

2. To the _____ eyes of his neighbors, Henry certainly looked like a madman; yet they treated him with kindness and understanding.

3. Mrs. Race may have been _____ by Henry's condition, but she made him breakfast with an almost

cheerful manner.

4. Phoebe's appearing to be alive was _____, a product only of Henry's mind.

5. Henry and Phoebe had in fact not been a _____ couple at all; if Phoebe threatened to leave Henry, she did it only jokingly.

6. It was decided to treat Henry _____ and let him wander, rather than send him to the county hospital, where the conditions were horrifying.

7. Henry, in his _____ condition, was unusually kindly and innocent, rather than dangerous or threatening.

8. In his _____ at Henry's story about Phoebe, Farmer Dodge could only stare after the man when he walked on down the road.

E. Close Reading and Vocabulary: The Importance of Adverbs

When an adverb joins together two complete statements, it expresses the relationship between the two statements. The meaning of the adverb therefore controls the meaning of the entire sentence. In the exercise below, finish the first statement with clause **a**, **b**, **c**, or **d**. Although all the statements in the exercise could be true, there is only *one* complete sentence in each group that accurately expresses the relationship between the two statements that make up the sentence.

1. Henry did not go to live with his daughter after Phoebe's death
   a. although he wanted to live with her
   b. because he was used to his home
   c. since his neighbors invited him to stay with them
   d. while his neighbors provided him with food

2. After Phoebe's death Henry was very unhappy for five months
   a. although he tried to interest himself in things like farming and reading the Bible
   b. until his neighbors began bringing him newspapers
   c. after he saw a figure that looked like Phoebe
   d. since he made coffee every morning and fried bacon every night
3. Phoebe came to Henry's bed and spoke to him
   a. before he saw her in the mist of the orchard
   b. when his hallucination had developed fully
   c. after he saw her as a shadow near the living room table
   d. until he begged her to stay
4. Matilda Race told Henry that she knew where Phoebe was
   a. since she could find Phoebe if anyone could
   b. although her eyes softened in sympathy
   c. when Henry began eating the food she brought him
   d. because she wanted to keep him there until her husband Jake came home to help
5. Henry was not placed in the county hospital for mad people
   a. until the police were informed of the case
   b. since he was harmless
   c. because the circle of his questioning grew wider and wider
   d. although he returned peaceably to his home every night
6. Henry's hallucination took the form of a search all over the countryside
   a. because in the past, after quarrels, Phoebe had threatened to leave him and go where he couldn't find her
   b. although he was sure she was still alive
   c. when he saw that no one was going to lock him up for behaving strangely
   d. after he became a common sight, and people got used to seeing him around

PART III (PAGES 124–128)

F. Language Activity: Answers as Riddles

Below is a list of answers. You are asked to make questions for which the answers are accurate. There may be more than one possible question for each answer. A paragraph number is given in case you need help. (How many can you do without returning to the story for a hint?) Work with a partner if possible.

Example:

On dusty roads and muddy ones. (paragraph 50)

Where did Henry walk on his travels?
or
What kinds of roads did Henry walk on?

1. In piles of grass or by the sides of cattle. (paragraph 51)
2. "O-o-o Phoebe! O-o-o Phoebe!" (paragraph 52)
3. This would surely tell him which way to go. (paragraph 53)
4. Red Cliff (paragraph 54)
5. These had made him only a shadow of his former self. (paragraph 56)
6. Young, beautiful, and girlish. (paragraphs 57 and 58)
7. His hat, his breath, and his mind. (paragraph 59)
8. Down below him, among the silver apple trees. (paragraph 59)
9. The pull of the world where love was young and Phoebe waited. (paragraph 60)
10. No one. (paragraph 61)

G. Discussion and Writing: "Respect for Old Henry"

In some ways, Henry Reifsneider is a comic character. Dreiser, in fact, is careful not to hide the funny side of Old Henry's hallucination. In the scenes with Farmer Dodge and Matilda Race, or when he throws his stick and turns around three times, we are likely to be amused as well as sympathetic. In the end, however, our sympathy for Henry is greater than our amusement. We grow to respect and even admire him, because in his search for his lost Phoebe, he shows certain qualities of character that we admire whenever we find them.

Re-read the following paragraph from the story:

> There were hours when his feet were sore and his legs tired. There were times when he would stop in the heat to wipe his forehead, or in the cold to beat his arms. Sometimes, after throwing his stick and finding it pointing to where he had just come from, he would shake his head wearily and philosophically. He would consider for a moment the confusion and disappointment of life, and his own strange fate. Then he would start energetically off again. His strange figure finally became known in the farthest corners of three or four counties.

Working with a partner (if possible), discuss the following questions. Together, plan a composition entitled "Respect for Old Henry." Write your own composition. Share the results with your partner.

What in the above paragraph wins our admiration for Henry? What are the strengths he shows us in his madness? What other admirable human qualities in Henry can you remember from other scenes in the story? (Think of the final scene among the trees on Red Cliff, for example.) Are these qualities worth less in Henry than they would be in a person who was not mad? Are they worth more? In short: Henry has lost his mind. The quality of reason is gone. What qualities remain?

Notes:

_____

_____